SARAH PAWLOWSKI

Crochet
FOR PLAY

80 Toys for Make-Believe

STACKPOLE BOOKS
Guilford, Connecticut

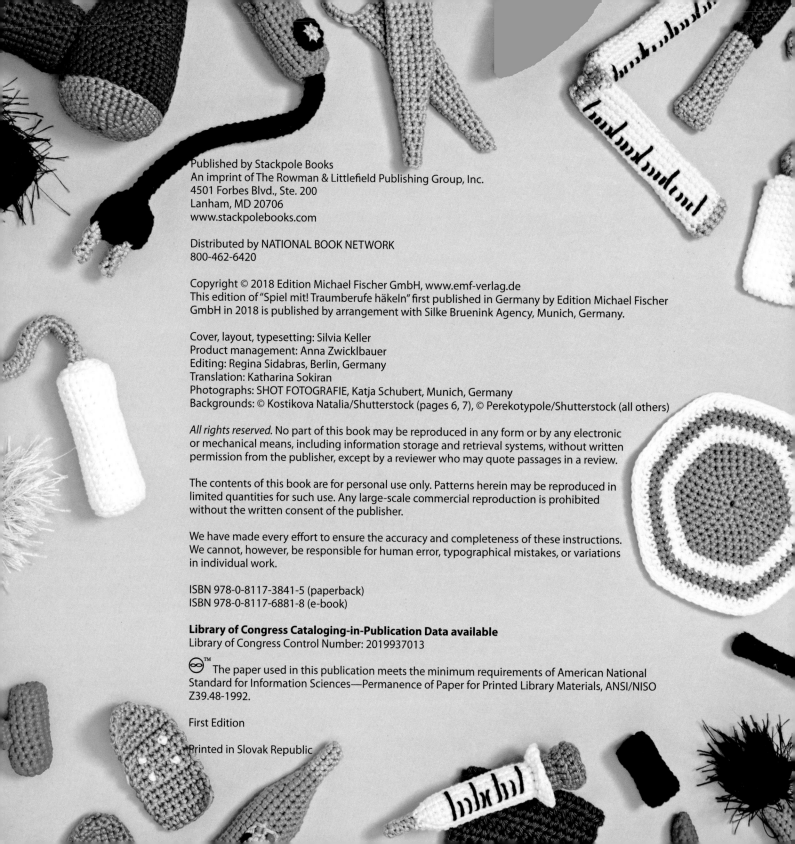

Published by Stackpole Books
An imprint of The Rowman & Littlefield Publishing Group, Inc.
4501 Forbes Blvd., Ste. 200
Lanham, MD 20706
www.stackpolebooks.com

Distributed by NATIONAL BOOK NETWORK
800-462-6420

Copyright © 2018 Edition Michael Fischer GmbH, www.emf-verlag.de
This edition of "Spiel mit! Traumberufe häkeln" first published in Germany by Edition Michael Fischer
GmbH in 2018 is published by arrangement with Silke Bruenink Agency, Munich, Germany.

Cover, layout, typesetting: Silvia Keller
Product management: Anna Zwicklbauer
Editing: Regina Sidabras, Berlin, Germany
Translation: Katharina Sokiran
Photographs: SHOT FOTOGRAFIE, Katja Schubert, Munich, Germany
Backgrounds: © Kostikova Natalia/Shutterstock (pages 6, 7), © Perekotypole/Shutterstock (all others)

ISBN 978-0-8117-3841-5 (paperback)
ISBN 978-0-8117-6881-8 (e-book)

Library of Congress Cataloging-in-Publication Data available
Library of Congress Control Number: 2019937013

⊖™ The paper used in this publication meets the minimum requirements of American National
Standard for Information Sciences—Permanence of Paper for Printed Library Materials, ANSI/NISO
Z39.48-1992.

First Edition

Printed in Slovak Republic

Contents

In the Garden 73

Preface

In 2015, I discovered my passion and talent for crocheting. Ever since then, hardly a day goes by when I don't grab a crochet hook. From hats to children's clothing, organizers, scarves, and shawls, to even a fully equipped toy kitchen and store—so far, I've hooked almost everything imaginable. Crocheting is a wonderful hobby, and being able to have a finished object, created with your own hands, after just a short amount of time is so rewarding!

Inspired by my daughter, who is four years old, and with a lot of attention to detail, I have designed the projects in this book. It will take you off into the world of dream jobs: doctor, handyperson, or hairdresser, for example. In this book, you can find patterns to make lots of exciting toy sets that girls and boys alike will be thrilled to play with. With just a crochet hook, yarn, and a small amount of stuffing, you will be making these beautiful toys in no time.

I wish you much fun when re-creating these projects!

Sarah Pawlowski

Basics

Everything needed to re-create the pictured props for eight dream jobs will be explained here, from tips for crocheting in the round and in rows to step-by-step instructions for all basic stitches and finishing details.

Before You Begin

Materials

For the crocheted pieces in this book, I've mostly used the cotton yarn **Camilla**, by **Woll Butt**, and in a few cases, **Catania**, by **Schachenmayr**. Both yarns have a yardage of 138 yd/125 m per 1.75 oz/50 g cotton and are ideally suited. If these are not available to you, choose a similarly plied, sport-weight cotton yarn of similar yardage/weight and gauge. In some instances, I've additionally used **Brazilia**, by **Schachenmayr**. Should this novelty yarn not be available, suitable alternatives are listed.

I have worked using **crochet hooks** in sizes **2.5 mm** and **3.0 mm**. If you do not have these sizes, try a US B-1 (2.25 mm), C-2 (2.75 mm), or D-3 (3.25 mm) hook. Finished size for most of these projects is not critical since they are toys, so a slight variation will not matter. Hook sizes used are individually listed in each pattern. If you want to substitute a different yarn than the one used for the sample, please refer to the ball band of the yarn, and choose the smallest hook size listed.

A significant number of crochet projects require **stuffing material**. I have used washable **polyester fiberfill**.

Since all crocheted pieces, with a few exceptions, are intentionally made of yarn and fiberfill only, they can later be laundered in the washing machine without any problems. I recommend placing them into a mesh wash bag in the delicate cycle. As an additional precaution, please always refer to the care instructions on the yarn label.

For closing openings in the crocheted pieces and weaving in ends, I've used a **tapestry needle** appropriate for the yarn weight. Additionally needed are **scissors**, a few **stitch markers**, the occasional **button,** and a small amount of **craft wire** or a few pieces of **pipe cleaners (chenille stems)**.

Brief Overview of Supplies

Most projects will use some or all of the following:

- » cotton yarn
- » novelty yarn
- » crochet hooks, 2.5 mm and/or 3.0 mm
- » polyester fiberfill
- » tapestry needle
- » stitch markers
- » scissors
- » pipe cleaners or craft wire
- » buttons

Typically, crochet patterns will list a gauge that shows how many rows and stitches are in a square of 4 in x 4 in/10 cm x 10 cm. For the projects in this book, I have intentionally omitted listing a gauge since the exact finished sizes of the items are not crucial. They should just be worked in a similar yarn with comparable yardage/weight and using a crochet hook in a matching size.

Important Tips

For every pattern, please read through all of the instructions before you begin, making sure to use the hook size and either the listed yarn or a similar one, and check whether any additional materials are required.

Crocheting in the Round

When crocheting in the round, each round starts with the indicated number of chains for height adjustment and is joined with a slip stitch into the first stitch of the round at the end. This is especially useful for pieces crocheted in several colors since it creates a clean color transition. Rounds worked in single crochet stitches always start with 1 chain for height adjustment, half double crochet rounds with 2 chains, and double crochet rounds with 3 chains. The correct number of height adjustment chains is always listed in the pattern.

Work is usually not turned when crocheting in the round, except when mentioned otherwise.

Starting with an adjustable magic ring: Form an adjustable magic ring, work the appropriate number of chains for height adjustment, and then work the listed number of stitches into the ring. End the round with a slip stitch into the first stitch.

Starting with a beginning chain: Work the required number of chains. If single crochets are to be worked in the first row after the chain, the last chain worked will be the chain for height adjustment. Crochet the required number of stitches into the chain, working either 2 or 3 stitches into the last chain as stated in the instructions. Now, continue into the unused loops on the other side of the chain. When you have reached the end of the round, join with a slip stitch into the first stitch of the round.

Working an edging around crocheted pieces: Sometimes, you will first crochet in turned rows, and later add an edging around the whole piece, usually in single crochet. In the first edging round, work as follows: After having completed the last row, do not turn your work. Chain 1 for height adjustment; then work the listed number of stitches on every side of the crocheted piece. The first and last stitch of the first and last row are the corner stitches. Into these corner stitches, work either 2 or 3 stitches, depending on the pattern. End the round with a slip stitch into the first stitch.

Working into Front and Back Loops

In some cases, you will work over the same round twice, first working only into one of the 2 loops of the stitch (either the back or front loop), and then into the unused loop of the same stitch during the second pass. These rounds will be marked "a" or "b" after the round number.

Spiral Rounds

All patterns in this book are written for joined rounds. If you prefer to crochet in spiral rounds instead, you can skip both the chain for height adjustment at the beginning, and the slip stitch at the end of the round. If doing so, place a piece of contrasting color yarn into the beginning of the round to make counting spiral rounds easier.

Crocheting Back and Forth in Rows

When crocheting in rows, work is turned at the end of each row. Before turning, here, too, the appropriate number of height adjustment chains has to be worked. To reach the required height, this will be 1 chain for single crochet rows, 2 chains for half double crochet rows, and 3 chains for double crochet rows. If, in a few cases, turning without turning chains is necessary, this, too, will be specially mentioned in the pattern.

Finishing Off and Hiding Ends

To finish off, work 1 additional chain, and break the yarn, leaving a tail of about 4 in/10 cm. Thread the end of the yarn through the last loop, and pull the loop closed. Using a tapestry needle in a matching size, weave the end of the yarn into the crocheted stitches.

For stuffed crocheted items, just pull the ending tail through to the inside of the item to hide.

If the pattern instructs to "break the yarn, leaving a long tail," then leave an end of about 20 in/50 cm. You will use it later for seaming or sewing on parts.

Seaming and Sewing

When seaming or sewing on crocheted parts, please use a tapestry needle and the project yarn, which creates a nearly invisible seam. This is best done using the long tail left when breaking the yarn.

Here, too, secure the end after seaming by making 1 or 2 sturdy knots; then weave in the end as described above.

Safety

Since the toys are meant to be used by children between 2 and 5 years of age, please make sure to firmly sew on small parts, and safely hide individual ends so that no small pieces can come undone later while playing.

Basic Stitches

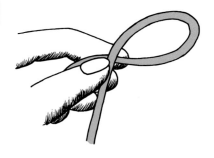 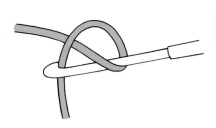 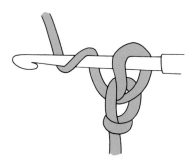

Beginning Slipknot

The beginning slipknot does not count as a stitch. Measure about 6 in/15 cm from the end of the yarn. Form the strand into a loop in this spot. Hold it in place with the thumb and middle finger of your left hand.

Lead the crochet hook through the yarn loop, grasp the working yarn coming from the ball, and pull it through the loop.

Slightly pull at the tail (short) end of the yarn to tighten the slipknot on the hook—you have completed the beginning slipknot.

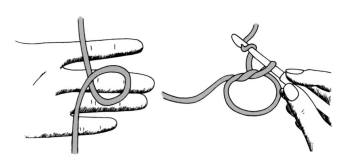 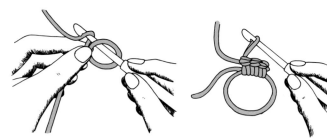

Magic Ring

Form the strand of yarn into a loop with the tail (short) end of the yarn pointing downward. Lead the ball end of the strand to the back over the index finger, and secure it between ring and middle finger.

Firmly hold the formed loop in place with thumb and index finger. Lead the crochet hook through the loop, grasp the working yarn, and draw it through the loop.

Grasp the working yarn once more, and draw it through the loop. This secures the ring.

Now you can crochet stitches as instructed. Always insert the hook into the void in the center of the ring. After all stitches have been worked, cinch the ring closed by pulling at the tail (short) end of the yarn.

Single Crochet (sc)

Insert the hook through the next stitch, and grasp the working yarn. There are now 2 loops on the hook.

Grasp the working yarn once more, and draw it through both loops on the hook at once. You have formed the first single crochet.

Insert the hook into the following stitch, and repeat the steps.

Half Double Crochet (hdc)

Lead the working yarn around the hook once (1 loop on hook).

Now, insert the hook into the following stitch, grasp the working yarn, and draw it through. There are now 3 loops on the hook.

Pull the working yarn through once more, and draw it through all 3 loops on the hook at once.

This is how the finished half double crochet stitch looks.

Double Crochet (dc)

As for a half double crochet, lead the working yarn over the hook once (yarn over). Now, insert the hook into the following stitch, grasp the working yarn, and draw it through. There are now 3 loops on the hook.

Pull the working yarn through once more, and draw it through the first 2 loops on the hook. Only 2 loops remain on the hook now.

Grasp the working yarn, and now draw it through the last 2 loops at once. You have finished the first double crochet stitch.

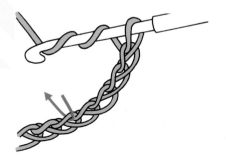
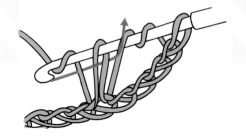
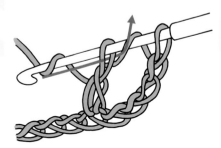

Treble Crochet

Lead the working yarn around the hook twice; then insert the hook into the fifth chain from the hook or stitch indicated in the pattern, and draw the working yarn through. There are now 4 loops on the hook.

Yarn over and pull the working yarn through the first 2 loops on the hook. 3 loops remain on the hook.

Grasp the working yarn again, and draw it through the first 2 loops on the hook. After this, only 2 loops remain on the hook. Yarn over and pull the working yarn through once more, drawing it through the last 2 loops at once. You have completed a treble crochet.

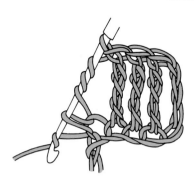
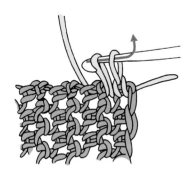
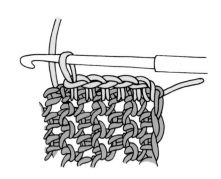

Triple Treble Crochet

The triple treble crochet is worked the same way as a treble—only here, before inserting the hook, the yarn is looped around the hook 3 times (3 yarn overs).

Slip Stitch

To work an edging around a piece, attach the yarn at one edge of the crocheted piece. Insert the hook under the turning chain of the adjoining row, pull up a loop from the working yarn, and then draw it through the loop on the hook (slip stitch formed).

This is how a crocheted slip stitch edging looks.

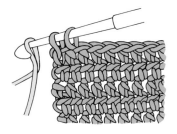 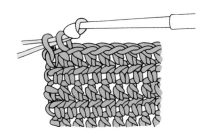 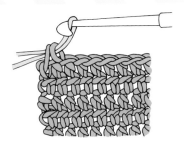

Joining New Working Yarn/Changing Colors in Rows

Work to the end of the row, but don't finish the last step of the last stitch in the old color; use the new color instead. To do this, draw a loop in the new color through ...

... and pull the yarn through the last 2 loops of the last stitch.

You are now ready to work the first turning chain for the next row in this new color.

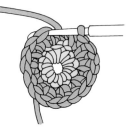   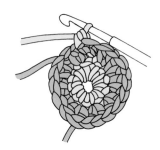

Changing Colors in Rounds

Crochet to the end of the round, but don't work the final slip stitch in the old color; use the new color instead.

To do this, place a loop in the new color on the hook, and pull it through both the stitch in the crocheted piece and the loop in the old color on the hook.

You are now ready to work the first height adjustment chain for the next row in this new color.

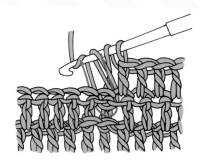

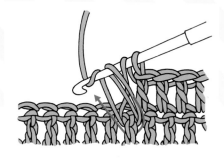

Raised Stitches

Raised stitches, or front or back post crochets, may be worked with all stitch types. The pictured samples show a back and front post double crochet.

Back post: Yarn over hook as usual; then, for a back post double crochet, insert the hook from the back to the front around the post of the stitch, instead of under both loops of the stitch.

Front post: For a front post double crochet, insert the hook from the front to the back around the post of the stitch of the previous row. Pull the working yarn through, and finish the double crochet as usual.

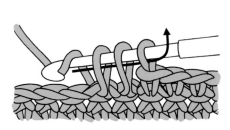

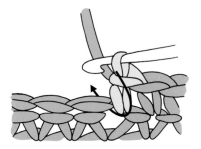

Increasing 1 single crochet

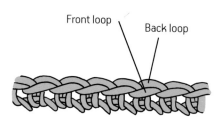

Front loop   Back loop

Decreasing Stitches

To decrease stitches, work them off together as one. For single crochets, work as follows: Insert the hook, as if to work a single crochet, through the next stitch, and pull the working yarn through, but do not finish the last step of this single crochet. Now, insert the hook into the following stitch, and pull the working yarn through once more. There are now 3 loops on the hook. Pull the working yarn through a third time, and draw it through all loops at once. The stitch count has been reduced; you have 1 single crochet fewer than before.

Increasing or Decreasing Stitches

Decreasing 1 stitch (dec 1) = crochet 2 stitches together, with 2 separate bases, leaving only 1 shared top.

Increasing 1 stitch (inc 1) = Make 2 stitches out of 1 by working 2 stitches into the same stitch, with 1 shared base and 2 separate tops.

Back and Front Loop of the Stitch

Some patterns will say to work into one loop of the stitch only. The illustration shows where the front and back loop can be found on the stitch.

Seaming & Embellishing

Basting

The basting stitch, also called a tacking or running stitch, is easy to work. Insert and exit the needle into and out of the crocheted fabric in evenly spaced steps along the required path. On the right side of the fabric, a line with gaps at uniform distances has formed.

Backstitch

The backstitch, also called a step stitch, is worked by going back through the end of the previous stitch. Bring the needle up through the fabric (1) and go back down through the fabric to the right of the exit point (2). The distance between exit point 1 and entry point 2 defines the stitch length. Now, exit to the left at a distance of 1 from the entry (3). Then, insert in point 1 again and exit a stitch length past 3. Repeat these steps for the desired length.

Tip

To ensure the realistic appearance of the crocheted objects, besides the actual crocheting, joining and embellishing also play an important role. Always do both with the working yarn from the crocheted project. Using thinner sewing thread would make the seam drown in the thicker crocheted fabric. A tapestry or embroidery needle appropriate for the yarn weight is the best choice. Please also refer to the detailed finishing instructions in each individual pattern, and carefully secure the ends after having finished seaming and embellishing.

Overcast Stitch

Pieces can be sewn together with the help of a darning needle using an overcast stitch. For an oversewn seam, place both pieces with their right sides facing each other, or wrong sides out. Secure the yarn, and draw the needle through the corresponding stitches on both pieces. Continue along the edges, going through both layers and finishing off by securely weaving in the end of the yarn.

Mattress Stitch

Mattress stitch is almost invisible on the right side of the fabric when completed. Place the 2 pieces to be joined flat next to each other, with their right sides facing up.

Inserting the tapestry needle between the first and second stitch in from the edge of the piece, lead the needle under 2 rows; then bring it back to the front between the first and the second stitch from the edge.

Go to the opposite edge, and lead the yarn through under 2 rows, repeating the steps in a zigzag path. When finished, lightly pull at the seaming yarn to tighten the seam. This has created an invisible seam.

French Knot

Wrap the yarn around the needle several times …

… insert it into the same point where it emerges from the fabric, and secure the yarn at the back of the work.

This is how a finished French knot will look.

Difficulty Levels & Abbreviations

Difficulty Levels

Patterns in this book are given three difficulty levels. Despite the great attention to detail in the designed items, I have made sure to write the instructions for re-creating them as simple as possible, and without using complicated stitches. This way, beginning crocheters, too, can enjoy them, and work their way up from easy projects to more advanced ones.

easy

medium

advanced

Abbreviations

bpsc = back post single crochet

ch = chain(s)

dc = double crochet

dec, dec'd = decrease, decreased

hdc = half double crochet(s)

inc, inc'd = increase, increased

prev = previous

rem = remaining

rep = repeat

rnd(s) = round(s)

sc = single crochet(s)

sc3tog = crochet 3 sc off together
(3 separate bases and 1 shared top)

sl-st = slip stitch(es)

st(s) = stitch(es)

tog = together

tr = triple/treble crochet(s)

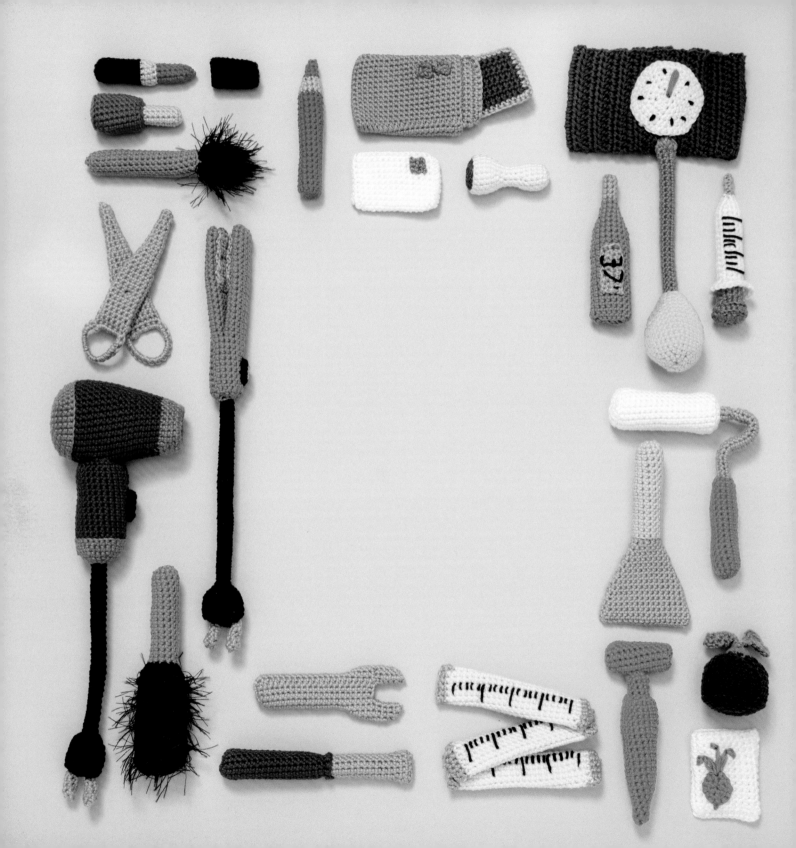

Projects

In the following chapters, you will find all kinds of props that boys and girls alike can use to role-play popular professions. Successfully re-creating these 60+ items will be a breeze with the detailed instructions provided.

AT THE Post Office

Stay in touch! Here, letters and parcels are postmarked, stamped, and sent on their way, using such tools as an envelope moistener and rubber stamp with ink pad. The mailbox wants to be emptied from time to time, too!

ENVELOPE

Materials

- » #2 fine weight cotton yarn; shown in Woll Butt Camilla, 100% cotton, 138 yd/125 m per 1.75 oz/50 g skein, in colors/amounts as follows:
  - » White, approx 27.6 yd/25 m, 0.35 oz/10 g
- » Crochet hook, 2.5 mm
- » Tapestry needle

Instructions

Work starts in the round. At the beginning of every rnd, ch1; at the end of every rnd, join with a sl-st into the first stitch of the rnd. Do not turn work.

In White, crochet a chain of 16.

Rnd 1: Work 1 sc in the 2nd ch from the hook, 1 sc in each of the following 13 chains, 2 sc in the last ch, and then continue into the unused loops on the other side of the chain: 1 sc in every ch. Join the rnd with 1 sl-st into the first stitch. (30 sts)

Rnds 2–10: 1 sc in every st of the prev rnd (30 sts). After having completed the last rnd, ch1, and turn work.

From here on, continue in back-and-forth rows with turning. End every row with ch1; then turn work.

Row 11: Working into the front loop of the stitch only: Dec 1, 1 sc in each of next 11 sts, dec 1. (13 sts)

Row 12: Dec 1, 1 sc in each of next 9 sts, dec 1. (11 sts)

Row 13: Dec 1, 1 sc in each of next 7 sts, dec 1. (9 sts)

Row 14: Dec 1, 1 sc in each of next 5 sts, dec 1. (7 sts)

Row 15: Dec 1, 1 sc in each of next 3 sts, dec 1. (5 sts)

Row 16: Dec 1, 1 sc in the next st, dec 1. (3 sts)

Row 17: Sc3tog the rem 3 sts. (1 st)

Finishing

- » For an open envelope, break the working yarn, secure, and weave in the end. For a closed envelope, break the working yarn, leaving a long tail, secure, and, using a tapestry needle and working in basting stitch, sew the seal flap to the envelope at the level of Rnds 5–10.

- » Crochet a postage stamp for the envelope (see page 23), and sew it to the top right corner of the envelope in basting stitch.

LARGE ENVELOPE & POSTAGE STAMP

Materials

Large Envelope

» #2 fine weight cotton yarn; shown in Woll Butt Camilla, 100% cotton, 138 yd/125 m per 1.75 oz/50 g skein, in colors/amounts as follows:
  » Caramel, approx 39.4 yd/37.5 m, 0.5 oz/15 g

Postage Stamp

» #2 fine weight cotton yarn; shown in Woll Butt Camilla, 100% cotton, 138 yd/125 m per 1.75 oz/50 g skein, in colors/amounts as follows:
  » Blue, remnant

For Both

» Crochet hook, 2.5 mm
» Tapestry needle

Instructions

LARGE ENVELOPE

Work starts in the round. At the beginning of every rnd, ch1; at the end of every rnd, join with a sl-st into the first stitch of the rnd. Do not turn work.

In Caramel, crochet a chain of 16.

Rnd 1: Work 1 sc in the 2nd ch from the hook, 1 sc in the following 13 chains, 2 sc in the last ch, and then continue into the unused loops on the other side of the chain: 1 sc in every ch. Join the rnd with 1 sl-st into the first stitch. (30 sts)

Rnds 2–21: 1 sc in every st of the prev rnd (30 sts). After having completed the last rnd, ch1, and turn work.
From here on, continue in back-and-forth rows with turning. End every row with ch1; then turn work.

Row 22: Working into the front loop of the stitch only: 1 sc in next 13 sts. (13 sts)

Rows 23–24: 1 sc in every st of the prev row. (13 sts)

Row 25: Dec 1, 1 sc in each of next 9 sts of the prev row, dec 1. (11 sts)

Finishing

» For a large open envelope, break the working yarn, secure, and weave in the end. For a large closed envelope, break the working yarn, leaving a long tail, secure and, using a tapestry needle and working in basting stitch, sew the seal flap to the envelope at the level of Rnd 19.

» Crochet 2 postage stamps for the large envelope, and sew them to the top right corner of the envelope in basting stitch.

POSTAGE STAMP

Work in back-and-forth rows with turning. End every row with ch1; then turn work.

In Blue, crochet a chain of 3.

Row 1: Work 1 sc in the 2nd ch from the hook, 1 sc in next ch. (2 sts)

Row 2: 1 sc in every st of the prev row. (2 sts)

Finishing

» Break the working yarn, secure the end, and attach the postage stamp to the envelope in basting stitch.

23

PACKAGE

Materials

- » #2 fine weight cotton yarn; shown in Woll Butt Camilla, 100% cotton, 138 yd/125 m per 1.75 oz/50 g skein, in colors/amounts as follows:
  - » Linen, approx 55.2 yd/50 m, 0.7 oz/20 g
- » Crochet hook, 2.5 mm
- » Polyester fiberfill
- » Tapestry needle

Instructions

PACKAGE BOTTOM

Work starts in back-and-forth rows with turning. End every row with ch1; then turn work.

In Linen, crochet a chain of 16.

Row 1: Work 1 sc in the 2nd ch from the hook, 1 sc in every following ch. (15 sts)
Rows 2–11: Work 1 sc in every st of the prev row (15 sts). After having completed the last row, don't turn work.
Continue as follows, working in rnds: Begin every rnd with ch1, end every rnd with 1 sl-st into the first st. Do not turn work.

Rnd 12: Crochet an edging around the whole piece, working 58 sc total: 10 sc at each of the 2 short sides, 13 sc at each of the 2 long sides, and 3 sc into each of the 4 corner sts. (58 sts)
Rnd 13: Working into the back loop of the stitch only: 1 sc in every st of the prev rnd. (58 sts)
Rnds 14–21: 1 sc in every st of the prev rnd. (58 sts)
Break the working yarn, and secure the end.

PACKAGE LID

Work Rows/Rnds 1–12 as for the package bottom; then break the yarn, leaving a long tail.

Finishing

- » Sew the sts of the package lid one to one to the sts of the package bottom, working in overcast stitch. When you have completed about half the seam, stuff the package with fiberfill. Seam to end, secure the yarn. Now, thread it to the middle of the topside, and string it around the package once lengthwise and once crosswise. Finish off by securing the end once more and hiding it on the inside.

MAILBOX

Materials

» #2 fine weight cotton yarn; shown in Schachenmayr Catania, 100% cotton, 138 yd/ 125 m per 1.75 oz/50 g skein, in colors/amounts as follows:
  » Sun, approx 1 skein
» Crochet hook, 2.5 mm
» Tapestry needle

Instructions

Work starts in back-and-forth rows with turning. End every row with ch1; then turn work.

In Sun, crochet a chain of 26.

Row 1: Work 1 sc in the 2nd ch from the hook, 1 sc in every following ch. (25 sts)

Rows 2–14: 1 sc in every st of the prev row (25 sts). After having completed the last row, don't turn work.

Continue as follows, working in rnds: Begin every rnd with ch1, end every rnd with 1 sl-st into the first st. Do not turn work.

Rnd 15: Crochet an edging around the whole piece, working 84 sc: 13 sc at each of the 2 short sides, 23 sc at each of the 2 long sides, and 3 sc into each of the 4 corner sts. (84 sts)

Rnd 16: Working into the back loop of the stitch only, 1 sc in every st of the prev rnd. (84 sts)

Rnds 17–30: 1 sc in every st of the prev rnd. (84 sts)

Rnd 31: 23 sc, ch16, skipping the next 14 sts of the prev rnd, 47 sc. (86 sts)

Rnd 32: 23 sc, 14 sc in ch-sp of the chain arc, 47 sc. (84 sts)

Rnds 33–37: 1 sc in every st of the prev rnd (84 sts). After having completed the last rnd, ch1, and turn work. From here on, continue in back-and-forth rows with turning. End every row with ch1; then turn work.

Row 38: Working into the front loop of the stitch only, 1 sc in each of next 25 sts. (25 sts)

Row 39: Inc 1, 1 sc in each of next 23 sts of the prev row, inc 1. (27 sts)

Row 40: Inc 1, 1 sc in each of next 25 sts of the prev row, inc 1. (29 sts)

Rows 41–53: 1 sc in every st of the prev row. (29 sts)

Finishing

» Break the working yarn, secure, and weave in the end. Pull the lid and the mail slot into the required shape.

ENVELOPE MOISTENER

Materials

- » #2 fine weight cotton yarn; shown in Woll Butt Camilla, 100% cotton, 138 yd/125 m per 1.75 oz/50 g skein, in colors/amounts as follows:
    - » Orange, approx 15.8 yd/12.5 m, 0.2 oz/5 g
    - » Green, approx 15.8 yd/12.5 m, 0.2 oz/5 g
- » Crochet hook, 2.5 mm
- » Polyester fiberfill
- » Tapestry needle

Instructions

Work in rnds. At the beginning of every rnd, ch1; at the end of every rnd, join with a sl-st into the first stitch of the rnd. Do not turn work.

Rnd 1: In Orange, work 6 sc into an adjustable magic ring. (6 sts)
Rnd 2: [Inc 1] 6 times. (12 sts)
Rnd 3: [1 sc, inc 1] 6 times. (18 sts)
Change to Green.

Rnd 4: [2 sc, inc 1] 6 times. (24 sts)
Rnd 5: Working into the back loop of the stitch only, 1 sc in every st of the prev rnd. (24 sts)
Rnd 6: [3 sc, inc 1] 6 times. (30 sts)
Rnds 7–8: 1 sc in every st of the prev rnd. (30 sts)
Rnd 9: Working into the back loop of the stitch only, [3 sc, dec 1] 6 times. (24 sts)
Rnd 10: [2 sc, dec 1] 6 times. (18 sts)

Rnd 11: [1 sc, dec 1] 6 times. (12 sts)
Stuff with fiberfill.
Rnd 12: [Dec 1] 6 times. (6 sts)

Finishing

- » Break the working yarn and, using a tapestry needle, thread through all 6 sts. Cinch to close the opening, secure the end, and weave it in on the inside.

PENCIL

Materials

» #2 fine weight cotton yarn; shown in Woll Butt Camilla, 100% cotton, 138 yd/125 m per 1.75 oz/50 g skein, in colors/amounts as follows:
  » Red, approx 15.8 yd/12.5 m, 0.2 oz/5 g
  » Linen, remnant
» Crochet hook, 2.5 mm
» Polyester fiberfill
» Tapestry needle

Instructions

Work in rnds. At the beginning of every rnd, ch1; at the end of every rnd, join with a sl-st into the first stitch of the rnd. Do not turn work.

Rnd 1: In Red, work 3 sc into an adjustable magic Ring. (3 sts)
Rnd 2: (Inc 1) 3 times. (6 sts)
Rnd 3: 1 sc in every st of the prev rnd. (6 sts)
Rnd 4: [1 sc, inc 1] 3 times. (9 sts)

Change to Linen.
Rnd 5: 1 sc in every st of the prev rnd. (9 sts)
Rnd 6: [2 sc, inc 1] 3 times. (12 sts)
Rnd 7: 1 sc in every st of the prev rnd. (12 sts)
Change to Red.
Rnds 8–25: 1 sc in every st of the prev rnd. (12 sts)
Stuff the pencil with fiberfill, and shape the tip.
Rnd 26: [Dec 1] 6 times. (6 sts)

Finishing

» Break the working yarn and, using a tapestry needle, thread through all 6 sts. Cinch to close the opening, secure the end, and weave it in on the inside.

RUBBER STAMP

Materials

» #2 fine weight cotton yarn; shown in Woll Butt Camilla, 100% cotton, 138 yd/125 m per 1.75 oz/50 g skein, in colors/amounts as follows:
  » Yellow, approx 15.8 yd/12.5 m, 0.2 oz/5 g
» #2 fine weight cotton yarn; shown in Schachenmayr Catania, 100% cotton, 138 yd/125 m per 1.75 oz/50 g skein, in colors/amounts as follows:
  » Jeans, remnant
» Crochet hook, 2.5 mm
» Polyester fiberfill

Instructions

Work in rnds. At the beginning of every rnd, ch1; at the end of every rnd, join with a sl-st into the first stitch of the rnd. Do not turn work.

Rnd 1: In Yellow, work 6 sc into an adjustable magic ring. (6 sts)
Rnd 2: [Inc 1] 6 times. (12 sts)
Rnds 3–5: 1 sc in every st of the prev rnd. (12 sts)
Rnd 6: [2 sc, dec 1] 3 times. (9 sts)
Rnds 7–9: 1 sc in every st of the prev rnd. (9 sts)
Rnd 10: [2 sc, inc 1] 3 times. (12 sts)
Rnd 11: [3 sc, inc 1] 3 times. (15 sts)
Rnd 12: [4 sc, inc 1] 3 times. (18 sts)
Rnds 13–15: 1 sc in every st of the prev rnd. (18 sts)
Change to Jeans.
Rnd 16: Working into the back loop of the stitch only, [1 sc, dec 1] 6 times. (12 sts)

Stuff the rubber stamp with fiberfill.
Rnd 17: [Dec 1] 6 times. (6 sts)

Finishing

» Break the working yarn and, using a tapestry needle, thread through all 6 sts. Cinch to close the opening, secure the end, and weave it in on the inside.

INK PAD

Materials

» #2 fine weight cotton yarn; shown in Woll Butt Camilla, 100% cotton, 138 yd/125 m per 1.75 oz/50 g skein, in colors/amounts as follows:
  » Grey, approx 15.8 yd/12.5 m, 0.2 oz/5 g
» #2 fine weight cotton yarn; shown in Schachenmayr Catania, 100% cotton, 138 yd/125 m per 1.75 oz/50 g skein, in colors/amounts as follows:
  » Jeans, approx 15.8 yd/12.5 m, 0.2 oz/5 g
» Crochet hook, 2.5 mm
» Tapestry needle

Instructions

Work in back-and-forth rows with turning. End every row with ch1; then turn work.

In Jeans, crochet a chain of 16.

Row 1: Work 1 sc in the 2nd ch from the hook, 1 sc in every following ch. (15 sts)
Rows 2–9: 1 sc in every st of the prev row. (15 sts)
Break the yarn, and secure the end.

In Grey, crochet a chain of 16, and repeat Rows 1–9. Do not break the working yarn in Grey.

Finishing

» Place both crocheted pieces atop each other, wrong sides facing each other with the Grey side on top, and crochet them together, working 1 rnd of sc as follows: Start with ch1, and then work 8 sc at each of the 2 short sides, 13 sc at each of the 2 long sides, and 3 sc into each of the 4 corner sts, join the rnd with 1 sl-st into the first st. (54 sts)

» Break the working yarn, secure, and weave in the tail.

AT THE
Hairdresser's

Shampoo, cut, and blow-dry, please! After a haircut, tresses are sculpted into any imaginable shape here: jauntily swept up with a hair dryer over a round brush, coiled onto curlers and held in place with styling clips, or turned smooth and silky with a straightening iron.

HAIR DRYER

Materials

» #2 fine weight cotton yarn; shown in Woll Butt Camilla, 100% cotton, 138 yd/125 m per 1.75 oz/50 g skein, in colors/amounts as follows:

  » Black, approx 39.4 yd/37.5 m, 0.5 oz/15 g

  » Marine, approx 39.4 yd/37.5 m, 0.5 oz/15 g

» Blue, approx 27.6 yd/25 m, 0.35 oz/10 g

» Grey, approx 15.8 yd/12.5 m, 0.2 oz/5 g

» Crochet hook, 2.5 mm

» Polyester fiberfill

» Tapestry needle

Work in rnds. At the beginning of every rnd, ch1; at the end of every rnd, join with a sl-st into the first stitch of the rnd. Do not turn work.

Hair Dryer

Rnd 1: In Blue, work 6 sc into an adjustable magic ring. (6 sts)
Rnd 2: [Inc 1] 6 times. (12 sts)
Rnd 3: [1 sc, inc 1] 6 times. (18 sts)
Rnd 4: [2 sc, inc 1] 6 times. (24 sts)
Rnd 5: [3 sc, inc 1] 6 times. (30 sts)
Rnd 6: [4 sc, inc 1] 6 times. (36 sts)
Rnds 7–8: 1 sc in every st of the prev rnd. (36 sts)
Change to Marine.
Rnd 9: Working into the back loop of the stitch only, 1 sc ea in every st of the prev rnd. (36 sts)
Rnds 10–15: 1 sc in every st of the prev rnd. (36 sts)
Rnd 16: [10 sc, dec 1] 3 times. (33 sts)
Rnds 17–18: 1 sc in every st of the prev rnd. (33 sts)
Rnd 19: [9 sc, dec 1] 3 times. (30 sts)
Rnds 20–21: 1 sc in every st of the prev rnd. (30 sts)
Rnd 22: [8 sc, dec 1] 3 times. (27 sts)
Rnd 23: 1 sc in every st of the prev rnd. (27 sts)
Change to Blue.
Rnd 24: 1 sc in every st of the prev rnd. (27 sts)
Rnd 25: [7 sc, dec 1] 3 times. (24 sts)
Rnd 26: 1 sc in every st of the prev rnd. (24 sts)
Rnd 27a: Working into the front loop of the stitch only, 1 sc in every st of the prev rnd. (24 sts)
Stuff the piece with fiberfill, and break the working yarn in Blue.

Join new working yarn in Black to the inner, un-used loop of the stitch, and continue as follows:

Rnd 27b: Working into the back loop of the stitch only, [2 sc, dec 1] 6 times. (18 sts)
Rnd 28: [1 sc, dec 1] 6 times. (12 sts)
Rnd 29: [Dec 1] 6 times. (6 sts)
Break the working yarn and, using a tapestry needle, thread through all 6 sts. Cinch to close the opening.
Secure all ends, and hide them on the inside.

Handle with Cord and Plug

Rnd 1: In Black, work 6 sc into an adjustable magic ring. (6 sts)
Rnd 2: [Inc 1] 6 times. (12 sts)
Rnd 3: [1 sc, inc 1] 6 times. (18 sts)
Rnd 4: Working into the back loop of the stitch only, 1 sc in every st of the prev rnd. (18 sts)
Rnds 5–7: 1 sc in every st of the prev rnd. (18 sts)
Rnd 8: [1 sc, dec 1] 6 times. (12 sts)
Stuff the piece with fiberfill.
Rnd 9: [Dec 1] 6 times. (6 sts)
Rnds 10–39: 1 sc in every st of the prev rnd. (6 sts)
Change to Blue.
Rnd 40: [Inc 1] 6 times. (12 sts)
Rnd 41: [1 sc, inc 1] 6 times. (18 sts)
Rnd 42: [2 sc, inc 1] 6 times. (24 sts)
Rnds 43–44: 1 sc in every st of the prev rnd. (24 sts)
Change to Marine.
Rnd 45: Working into the back loop of the stitch only, 1 sc in every st of the prev rnd. (24 sts)
Rnds 46–57: 1 sc in every st of the prev rnd. (24 sts)
Break the working yarn, leaving a long tail.

Plug Pins (make 2)

Rnd 1: In Grey, work 4 sc into an adjustable magic ring. (4 sts)

Rnds 2–5: 1 sc in every st of the prev rnd. (4 sts)
Break the working yarn, leaving a long tail.

Switch

Rnd 1: In Black, work 6 sc into an adjustable magic ring. (6 sts)
Rnd 2: [Inc 1] 6 times. (12 sts)
Rnd 3: Working into the back loop of the stitch only, 1 sc in every st of the prev rnd. (12 sts)
Break the working yarn, leaving a long tail.

Finishing

» Sew the 2 plug pins side by side to the plug at the end of the cord in overcast stitch at the level of Rnds 1–3. Insert a small amount of stuffing into the switch, and sew it onto the handle in overcast stitch at the level of Rnds 48–52. Now, stuff the handle with fiberfill, too, and sew it to the barrel of the hair dryer in overcast stitch at the level of Rnds 10–16.

Tip

The length of the cord can be adjusted as needed by working more sc rnds in Black for the cord after Rnd 39. However, please ensure that the cord will still be short enough not to pose a strangulation hazard to the child!

If you want to omit the cord and plug, start with a magic ring in Blue, sc 6 into the ring, and then continue working from Rnd 40 of the handle instructions.

STRAIGHTENING IRON

Materials

» #2 fine weight cotton yarn; shown in Woll Butt Camilla, 100% cotton, 138 yd/125 m per 1.75 oz/50 g skein, in colors/amounts as follows:

  » Emerald, approx 27.6 yd/25 m, 0.35 oz/10 g

  » Black, approx 27.6 yd/25 m, 0.35 oz/10 g

» Grey, approx 15.8 yd/12.5 m, 0.2 oz/5 g

» Crochet hook, 2.5 mm

» Polyester fiberfill

» Tapestry needle

Straightening Iron with Cord and Plug

Work in rnds. At the beginning of every rnd, ch1, at the end of every rnd, join with a sl-st into the first stitch of the rnd. Do not turn work.

Rnd 1: In Emerald, work 6 sc into an adjustable magic ring. (6 sts)
Rnd 2: [Inc 1] 6 times. (12 sts)
Rnds 3–20: 1 sc in every st of the prev rnd. (12 sts)
Break the working yarn, and secure the end.

Make a second piece the same way, but this time, leave a long tail. Place the 2 crocheted pieces atop each other, wrong sides facing, and, using the tail, sew them together in overcast stitch over a width of 3 adjoining sts.

Join new working yarn in Emerald, and crochet over the remaining 18 sts of the 2 joined pieces as follows:

Rnds 21–30: 1 sc in every st of the prev rnd. (18 sts)
Rnd 31: [1 sc, dec 1] 6 times. (12 sts)
Lightly stuff the straightening iron with fiberfill.
Rnd 32: [Dec 1] 6 times. (6 sts)
Change to Black.
Rnd 33: Working into the back loop of the stitch only, 1 sc in every st of the prev rnd. (6 sts)
Rnds 34–63: 1 sc in every st of the prev rnd. (6 sts)
Rnd 64: [Inc 1] 6 times. (12 sts)
Rnd 65: [1 sc, inc 1] 6 times. (18 sts)

Rnds 66–69: 1 sc in every st of the prev rnd. (18 sts)
Rnd 70: Working into the back loop of the stitch only, [1 sc, dec 1] 6 times. (12 sts)
Stuff Rnds 64–70 with fiberfill.
Rnd 71: [Dec 1] 6 times. (6 sts)
Break the working yarn and, using a tapestry needle, thread through all 6 sts. Cinch to close the opening.

Secure all ends, and hide them on the inside.

Plug Pins (make 2)

Work in rnds. At the beginning of every rnd, ch1, at the end of every rnd, join with a sl-st into the first stitch of the rnd. Do not turn work.
Rnd 1: In Grey, work 4 sc into an adjustable magic ring. (4 sts)
Rnds 2–5: 1 sc in every st of the prev rnd. (4 sts)
Break the working yarn, leaving a long tail.

Switch

Work in rnds. At the beginning of every rnd, ch1, at the end of every rnd, join with a sl-st into the first stitch of the rnd. Do not turn work.
Rnd 1: In Grey, work 6 sc into an adjustable magic ring. (6 sts)
Change to Black.
Rnd 2: [Inc 1] 6 times. (12 sts)
Break the working yarn, leaving a long tail.

Heating Plates (make 2)

Work in back-and-forth rows with turning. End every row with ch1; then turn work.
In Grey, crochet a chain of 5.
Row 1: Work 1 sc in the 2nd ch from the hook, 1 sc in every following ch. (4 sts)
Rows 2–10: 1 sc in every st of the prev row. (4 sts)
Break the working yarn, leaving a long tail.

Finishing

» Sew the 2 plug pins side by side to the plug at the cord's end in overcast stitch at the level of Rows 70–71. Sew the switch to the middle of the straightening iron in overcast stitch at the level of Row 26. Working in basting stitch, sew the 2 heating plates to the 2 inner sides of the straightening iron at the level of Rows 3–13. Secure all ends, and hide them on the inside.

Tip

The length of the cord can be adjusted as needed by working more sc rnds in Black for the straightening iron after Rnd 36. However, please ensure that the cord will still be short enough not to pose a strangulation hazard to the child!

If you want to omit the cord and plug, finish work on the straightening iron after Rnd 32, thread the tail through all 6 sts, and cinch the remaining opening closed.

AT THE HAIRDRESSER'S

COMB

Materials

- » #2 fine weight cotton yarn; shown in Woll Butt Camilla, 100% cotton, 138 yd/125 m per 1.75 oz/50 g skein, in colors/amounts as follows:
  - » Marine, approx 27.6 yd/25 m, 0.35 oz/10 g
- » Crochet hook, 2.5 mm
- » Tapestry needle

Instructions

Work in rnds. At the beginning of every rnd, ch1; at the end of every rnd, join with a sl-st into the first stitch of the rnd. Do not turn work.

Handle

Rnd 1: In Marine, work 6 sc into an adjustable magic ring. (6 sts)

Rnd 2: [Inc 1] 6 times. (12 sts)

Rnds 3–15: 1 sc in every st of the prev rnd. (12 sts)

Rnd 16: [2 sc, dec 1] 3 times. (9 sts)

Rnds 17–30: 1 sc in every st of the prev rnd. (9 sts)

Rnd 31: [1 sc, dec 1] 3 times. (6 sts)

Break the working yarn and, using a tapestry needle, thread the tail through all 6 sts, and cinch the remaining opening closed. Secure the end, and hide it on the inside.

Teeth (make 4)

Rnd 1: In Marine, work 4 sc into an adjustable magic ring. (4 sts)

Rnds 2–7: 1 sc in every st of the prev rnd. (4 sts)

Break the working yarn, leaving a long tail, and thread the tail through all 4 sts with a tapestry needle. Cinch to close the opening, and thread the tail on the inside to Rnd 1.

Finishing

- » Sew the 4 teeth to the side of the shaft in overcast stitch at the level of Rnds 16–18, 20–22, 24–26, and 28–30. Now, secure all ends, and hide them on the inside of the comb.

ROUND HAIRBRUSH

Materials

- » #2 fine weight cotton yarn; shown in Woll Butt Camilla, 100% cotton, 138 yd/125 m per 1.75 oz/50 g skein, in colors/amounts as follows:
  - » Pink, approx 27.6 yd/25 m, 0.35 oz/10 g
  - » Black, approx 27.6 yd/25 m, 0.35 oz/10 g
- » Eyelash yarn, #4 medium weight; shown in Schachenmayr Brazilia, 100% polyester, 99 yd/90 m per 1.75 oz/50 g skein
  - » Black, approx 11.3 yd/9 m, 0.2 oz/5 g
- » Crochet hook, 2.5 mm
- » Polyester fiberfill
- » Tapestry needle

Instructions

Work in rnds. At the beginning of every rnd, ch1, at the end of every rnd, join with a sl-st into the first stitch of the rnd. Do not turn work.

Rnd 1: In Pink, work 6 sc into an adjustable magic ring. (6 sts)
Rnd 2: [Inc 1] 6 times. (12 sts)
Rnds 3–17: 1 sc in every st of the prev rnd. (12 sts)
Change to Black.
Rnd 18: [1 sc, inc 1] 6 times. (18 sts)
Rnd 19: [2 sc, inc 1] 6 times. (24 sts)

Stuff the handle with fiberfill.
Rnd 20: Working into the back loop of the stitch only, 1 sc in every st of the prev rnd. (24 sts)
Rnds 21–34: 1 sc in every st of the prev rnd. (24 sts)
Rnd 35: Working into the back loop of the stitch only, [2 sc, dec 1] 6 times. (18 sts)
Stuff the remaining part with fiberfill, too.
Rnd 36: [1 sc, dec 1] 6 times. (12 sts)
Rnd 37: [Dec 1] 6 times. (6 sts)
Break the working yarn, leaving a tail. Now, using a tapestry needle, thread the tail through all 6 sts. Cinch to close the opening. Secure the end of the yarn, and hide the tail on the inside of the hairbrush.

Finishing

- » Using eyelash yarn in Black, embroider in running stitch over a width of 4 sts onto Rnds 21, 25, 30, and 34. Repeat the stitching another 5 times for every rnd. Now, secure the ends of the yarn, and pull individual strands into shape.

CURLERS

Materials

» #2 fine weight cotton yarn; shown in Woll Butt Camilla, 100% cotton, 138 yd/125 m per 1.75 oz/50 g skein, in pastel colors/amounts as follows:
  » Light Green, approx 15.8 yd/12.5 m, 0.2 oz/5 g
  » Orange, approx 15.8 yd/12.5 m, 0.2 oz/5 g
  » Lavender, approx 15.8 yd/12.5 m, 0.2 oz/5 g
» Crochet hook, 2.5 mm
» Tapestry needle

Instructions

Work in rnds. At the beginning of every rnd, ch1, at the end of every rnd, join with a sl-st into the first stitch of the rnd. Do not turn work.

Ch15 in the desired color, and join the chain into the round with a sl-st into the first chain.

Rnd 1: Work 15 sc around the chain ring. (15 sts)
Rnds 2–11: Work 1 sc in every st of the prev rnd. (15 sts)

Finishing

» Break the working yarn, secure the end, and weave in between the sts with a tapestry needle.

STYLING CLIPS

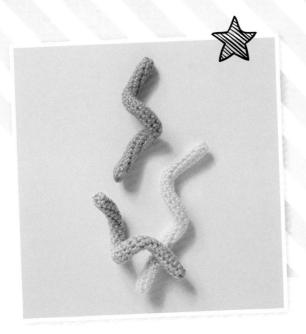

Materials

» #2 fine weight cotton yarn; shown in Woll Butt Camilla, 100% cotton, 138 yd/125 m per 1.75 oz/50 g skein, in bright colors/amounts as follows:
  » Turquoise, approx 15.8 yd/12.5 m, 0.2 oz/5 g
  » Yellow, approx 15.8 yd/12.5 m, 0.2 oz/5 g
  » Pink, approx 15.8 yd/12.5 m, 0.2 oz/5 g
» Crochet hook, 2.5 mm
» Tapestry needle
» Pipe cleaners or craft wire
» Adhesive tape

Instructions

Work in rnds. At the beginning of every rnd, ch1; at the end of every rnd, join with a sl-st into the first stitch of the rnd. Do not turn work.

Rnd 1: In the desired color, work 6 sc into an adjustable magic ring. (6 sts)
Rnds 2–30: 1 sc in every st of the prev rnd. (6 sts)
Break the working yarn.

Finishing

» Shorten a piece of craft wire or a pipe cleaner to a length of about 4 in/10 cm (the wire should be slightly shorter than the crocheted piece). Bend the ends, and wrap them with adhesive tape for protection to prevent any sharp points. Push the wire into the crocheted piece. Now, thread the yarn tail through all 6 sts, and cinch the remaining opening closed. Check once more that both ends are firmly sealed. Secure the end, and hide the tail on the inside.

SCISSORS

Materials

» #2 fine weight cotton yarn; shown in Woll Butt Camilla, 100% cotton, 138 yd/125 m per 1.75 oz/50 g skein, in colors/amounts as follows:
  » Grey, approx 27.6 yd/25 m, 0.35 oz/10 g
» Crochet hook, 2.5 mm
» Tapestry needle

Instructions

Scissor Blades (make 2)

Work in rnds. At the beginning of every rnd, ch1; at the end of every rnd, join with a sl-st into the first stitch of the rnd. Do not turn work.

In Grey, ch20, and join into the round with a sl-st into the first chain.

Rnd 1: Work 20 sc around the ring. (20 sts)
Rnd 2: Working into the back loop of the stitch only, 1 sc into the first 6 sts, ch1, turn work; working into the front loops of the same sts, 6 sc, join into the round with a sl-st into the first st. (13 sts)

Rnd 3: 1 sc in every st of the prev rnd, except for the ch in the middle, which gets skipped. (12 sts)
Rnds 4–12: 1 sc in every st of the prev rnd. (12 sts)
Rnd 13: [Dec 1, 4 sc] 2 times. (10 sts)
Rnds 14–15: 1 sc in every st of the prev rnd. (10 sts)
Rnd 16: [Dec 1, 3 sc] 2 times. (8 sts)
Rnds 17–18: 1 sc in every st of the prev rnd. (8 sts)
Rnd 19: [Dec 1, 2 sc] 2 times. (6 sts)
Rnds 20–21: 1 sc in every st of the prev rnd. (6 sts)

Rnd 22: [Dec 1, 1 sc] 2 times. (4 sts)
Rnds 23–24: 1 sc in every st of the prev rnd. (4 sts)

Break the working yarn, and thread the tail through all 4 sts with a tapestry needle. Cinch the remaining opening closed. Secure the end of the yarn, and hide the tail on the inside of the scissor blade.

Finishing

» Place both scissor blades diagonally over each other, and attach firmly with several running stitches at the level of Rnd 8 over the width of 1 st.

HAIR BAND WITH FLOWERS

Materials

» #2 fine weight cotton yarn; shown in Woll Butt Camilla, 100% cotton, 138 yd/125 m per 1.75 oz/50 g skein, in colors/amounts as follows:
  » Pink, approx 39.4 yd/37.5 m, 0.5 oz/15 g
  » White, approx 15.8 yd/12.5 m, 0.2 oz/5 g
» Crochet hooks, 2.5 mm and 3.0 mm
» Tapestry needle

Instructions

Hair Band

Work in back-and-forth rows with turning. End every row with ch1; then turn work.

In Pink and with the 2.5 mm hook, crochet a chain of 6.

Row 1: Work 1 sc in the 2nd ch from the hook, 1 sc in every following ch. (5 sts)
Rows 2–100: Working into the back loop of the stitch only, 1 sc in every st of the prev row. (5 sts)
Row 101: Place the 2 ends of the band together, and crochet Rows 1 and 101 together with 5 sl-sts worked through the back loop of the sts (5 sts). Make sure that the crocheted band is not twisted.

Tip

A hair band made using the listed yarn and hook size will fit a head circumference of approx 20 in/50 cm. You can adjust the size to the head circumference of your child by working more or fewer rows, whereby 2 rows equal approx 0.4 in/1 cm.

Flower

Work in rnds. At the beginning of every rnd, ch1, and at the end of every round, join with a sl-st into the first stitch of the rnd. Do not turn work.

Rnd 1: In White and using the 2.5 mm hook, work the following sts into an adjustable magic ring: [1 sc, 1 hdc, 1 dc, 1 tr, 1 dc, 1 hdc] 5 times, join into the round with a sl-st into the first st. (30 sts)
Cinch the ring closed.

Following the same instructions, make another flower, this time using the 3.0 mm hook so it will turn out slightly larger.

Finishing

» Use the yarn tails to sew the flowers to the headband. Secure the yarn, and weave in the ends.

FOR LITTLE
Painters

Caution, wet paint! Spackling is followed by a fresh coat of paint. Paint is mixed to shade in the can. Large surfaces are tackled with a paint roller and bucket grid. A paintbrush is used for nooks and crannies.

PAINT CAN

Materials

- » #2 fine weight cotton yarn; shown in Woll Butt Camilla, 100% cotton, 138 yd/125 m per 1.75 oz/50 g skein, in colors/amounts as follows:
  - » White, approx 86.7 yd/75 m, 1.1 oz/30 g
  - » Additional color of choice (shown in Red), approx 27.6 yd/25 m, 0.35 oz/10 g
- » Crochet hook, 3.0 mm
- » Polyester fiberfill
- » Tapestry needle

Instructions

Work in rnds. At the beginning of every rnd, ch1; at the end of every rnd, join with a sl-st into the first stitch of the rnd. Do not turn work.

Rnd 1: In White, work 6 sc into an adjustable magic ring. (6 sts)
Rnd 2: [Inc 1] 6 times. (12 sts)
Rnd 3: [1 sc, inc 1] 6 times. (18 sts)
Rnd 4: [2 sc, inc 1] 6 times. (24 sts)
Rnd 5: [3 sc, inc 1] 6 times. (30 sts)
Rnd 6: [4 sc, inc 1] 6 times. (36 sts)
Rnd 7: [5 sc, inc 1] 6 times. (42 sts)
Rnd 8: [6 sc, inc 1] 6 times. (48 sts)
Rnd 9: Working into the back loop of the stitch only, 1 sc in every st of the prev rnd. (48 sts)
Rnds 10–24: 1 sc in every st of the prev rnd. (48 sts)
Rnd 25a: Working into the front loop of the stitch only, 1 sc in every st of the prev rnd. (48 sts)

The following 2 rnds are worked in the sts of Rnd 25a:
Next 2 rounds: 1 sc in every st of the prev rnd. (48 sts)
Break the working yarn, leaving a long tail; then fold the edge (last 3 rounds) over outward, so that the unused back loops of the sts from Rnd 25a point inward. Using the long tail and a tapestry needle and working in basting stitch, sew on the edge at the level of Rnd 22.

Join new working yarn in Red to Rnd 24, and continue as follows, working into the inner, unused loops of the sts:
Rnd 25b: Working into the back loop of the stitch only, [6 sc, dec 1] 6 times (42 sts) while also adding paint drips in as many spots as desired, as follows: Ch11, 1 sc in the 2nd ch from the hook, 1 sc in every following ch (10 sts). **Or** ch8, 1 sc in the 2nd ch from the hook, 1 sc in every following ch. (7 sts)

Now, fold the paint drips outward, and in the next rnd, continue over the 42 sc only.
Rnd 26: [5 sc, dec 1] 6 times. (36 sts)
Rnd 27: [4 sc, dec 1] 6 times. (30 sts)
Rnd 28: [3 sc, dec 1] 6 times. (24 sts)
Rnd 29: [2 sc, dec 1] 6 times. (18 sts)
Stuff the can with fiberfill.
Rnd 30: [1 sc, dec 1] 6 times. (12 sts)
Rnd 31: [Dec 1] 6 times. (6 sts)

Finishing

- » Break the working yarn, leaving a long tail, thread through all 6 sts with a tapestry needle, and cinch the opening closed. Using the yarn tail and working in basting stitch, attach the paint drips on the outside of the paint can.

PUTTY KNIFE

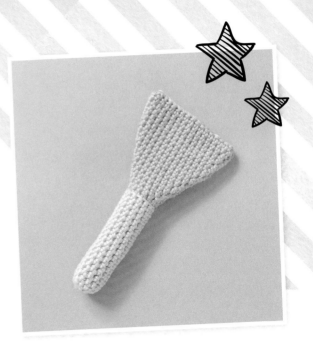

Materials

» #2 fine weight cotton yarn; shown in Woll Butt Camilla, 100% cotton, 138 yd/125 m per 1.75 oz/50 g skein, in colors/amounts as follows:
   » Linen, approx 27.6 yd/25 m, 0.35 oz/10 g
   » Grey, approx 27.6 yd/25 m, 0.35 oz/10 g
» Crochet hook, 2.5 mm
» Polyester fiberfill
» Tapestry needle

Instructions

Work in rnds. At the beginning of every rnd, ch1; at the end of every rnd, join with a sl-st into the first stitch of the rnd. Do not turn work.

Rnd 1: In Linen, work 6 sc into an adjustable magic ring. (6 sts)
Rnd 2: [Inc 1] 6 times. (12 sts)
Rnds 3–17: 1 sc in every st of the prev rnd. (12 sts)
Stuff the piece with fiberfill.
Change to Grey.
Rnd 18: Working into the back loop of the stitch only, 1 sc in every st of the prev rnd. (12 sts)
Rnd 19: [Inc 1, 5 sc] 2 times. (14 sts)

Rnd 20: 1 sc, inc 1, 6 sc, inc 1, 5 sc. (16 sts)
Rnd 21: 2 sc, inc 1, 7 sc, inc 1, 5 sc. (18 sts)
Rnd 22: 2 sc, inc 1, 8 sc, inc 1, 6 sc. (20 sts)
Rnd 23: 3 sc, inc 1, 9 sc, inc 1, 6 sc. (22 sts)
Rnd 24: 4 sc, inc 1, 10 sc, inc 1, 6 sc. (24 sts)
Rnd 25: 4 sc, inc 1, 11 sc, inc 1, 7 sc. (26 sts)
Rnd 26: 5 sc, inc 1, 12 sc, inc 1, 7 sc. (28 sts)
Rnd 27: 5 sc, inc 1, 13 sc, inc 1, 8 sc. (30 sts)
Rnd 28: 1 sc in every st of the prev rnd. (30 sts)
Rnd 29: 6 sc, inc 1, 14 sc, inc 1, 8 sc. (32 sts)
Rnd 30: 1 sc in every st of the prev rnd. (32 sts)
Rnd 31: 6 sc, inc 1, 15 sc, inc 1, 9 sc. (34 sts)
Rnd 32: 1 sc in every st of the prev rnd. (34 sts)
Break the working yarn, leaving a long tail.

Finishing

» Using the long tail and a tapestry needle, going through the outer loops of sts only, sew the sts of the remaining opening closed 1 to 1 in overcast stitch, while the sts with increases are located at the outer edges of the crocheted piece.

PAINTBRUSH

Materials

- » #2 fine weight cotton yarn; shown in Woll Butt Camilla, 100% cotton, 138 yd/125 m per 1.75 oz/50 g skein, in colors/amounts as follows:
  - » Linen, approx 27.6 yd/25 m, 0.35 oz/10 g
  - » Red, remnant
  - » Grey, remnant
- » Eyelash yarn, #4 medium weight; shown in Schachenmayr Brazilia, 100% polyester, 99 yd/90 m per 1.75 oz/50 g skein, in colors/amounts as follows:
  - » Camel, approx 11.3 yd/9 m, 0.2 oz/5 g (or Woll Butt Camilla in Yellow)
- » Crochet hook, 2.5 mm
- » Tapestry needle

Instructions

Work starts in back-and-forth rows with turning. End every row with ch1; then turn work.

In Grey, crochet a chain of 8.

Row 1: Work 1 sc in the 2nd ch from the hook, 1 sc in every following ch. (7 sts)

Row 2: 1 sc in every st of the prev row. (7 sts) Do not turn at the end of this row.

Continue as follows, working in rnds: At the beginning of every rnd, ch1; at the end of every rnd, join with a sl-st into the first stitch of the rnd. Do not turn work.

Rnd 3: Crochet an edging around the whole piece: 24 sc total, of these 1 sc at each side, 5 sc at each of top and bottom edge, and 3 sc into each of the 4 corner sts. (24 sts)

Rnd 4: Working into the back loop of the stitch only, 1 sc in every st of the prev rnd. (24 sts)

Rnds 5—6: 1 sc in every st of the prev rnd. (24 sts)

Change to Linen.

Rnd 7: Working into the back loop of the stitch only, 1 sc in every st of the prev rnd. (24 sts)

Rnd 8: 1 sc in every st of the prev rnd. (24 sts)

Rnd 9: [Dec 1, 10 sc] 2 times. (22 sts)

Rnd 10: [Dec 1, 9 sc] 2 times. (20 sts)

Rnd 11: [Dec 1, 8 sc] 2 times. (18 sts)

Rnd 12: [Dec 1, 7 sc] 2 times. (16 sts)

Rnds 13—22: 1 sc in every st of the prev rnd. (16 sts)

Rnd 23: [6 sc, dec 1] 2 times. (14 sts)

Rnd 24: [5 sc, dec 1] 2 times. (12 sts)

Stuff the piece with fiberfill, and shape it. Change to Red.

Rnd 25: [Dec 1, 4 sc] 2 times. (10 sts)

Rnd 26: [Dec 1, 3 sc] 2 times. (8 sts)

Rnd 27: [Dec 1, 2sc] 2 times. (6 sts)

Fill the remaining part with fiberfill, too. Break the working yarn and, using a tapestry needle, thread through all 6 sts. Cinch to close the opening. Secure the end of the yarn, and hide the tail on the inside of the paintbrush.

Finishing

- » In eyelash yarn (Schachenmayr Brazilia in Camel) and with a tapestry needle, sew little loops to Rows 1—3 in running stitch, to look like bristles sticking out. As an alternative, knot on short lengths of cotton yarn (Woll Butt Camilla in Yellow), and then unply the unattached ends for a frayed look.

PAINT ROLLER

Materials

» #2 fine weight cotton yarn; shown in Woll Butt Camilla, 100% cotton, 138 yd/125 m per 1.75 oz/50 g skein, in colors/amounts as follows:
  » White, approx 15.8 yd/12.5 m, 0.2 oz/5 g
  » Grey, approx 15.8 yd/12.5 m, 0.2 oz/5 g
  » Red, approx 15.8 yd/12.5 m, 0.2 oz/5 g
» Crochet hook, 2.5 mm
» Polyester fiberfill
» Tapestry needle
» Pipe cleaners or craft wire
» Adhesive tape

Instructions

Work in rnds. At the beginning of every rnd, ch1; at the end of every rnd, join with a sl-st into the first stitch of the rnd. Do not turn work.

Roller Cover

Rnd 1: In White, work 6 sc into an adjustable magic ring. (6 sts)
Rnd 2: [Inc 1] 6 times. (12 sts)
Rnd 3: [1 sc, inc 1] 6 times. (18 sts)
Rnd 4: Working into the back loop of the stitch only, 1 sc in every st of the prev rnd. (18 sts)
Rnds 5—20: 1 sc in every st of the prev rnd. (18 sts)
Rnd 21: Working into the back loop of the stitch only, [1 sc, dec 1] 6 times. (12 sts)
Stuff with fiberfill.
Rnd 22: [Dec 1] 6 times. (6 sts)
Change to Grey.

Rnd 23: Working into the front loop of the stitch only, 1 sc in every st of the prev rnd. (6 sts)
Rnd 24: 1 sc in every st of the prev rnd. (6 sts)
Break the working yarn.

Handle

Rnd 1: In Red, work 6 sc into an adjustable magic ring. (6 sts)
Rnd 2: [Inc 1] 6 times. (12 sts)
Rnds 3—17: 1 sc in every st of the prev rnd. (12 sts)
Stuff with fiberfill.
Rnd 18: [2 sc, dec 1] 3 times. (9 sts)
Change to Grey.
Rnd 19: Working into the back loop of the stitch only, [1 sc, dec 1] 3 times. (6 sts)
Rnds 20—35: 1 sc in every st of the prev rnd. (6 sts)
Break the working yarn, leaving a long tail.

Finishing

» Shorten a piece of pipe cleaner or craft wire to a length of approx 3.2 in/8 cm (the piece of wire should have the same length as the grey crocheted part). Bend the ends, and wrap them with adhesive tape for protection, to prevent any sharp points. Insert the wire into the crocheted piece.

» Now, working in overcast stitch, sew Rnd 24 of the roller cover to Rnd 35 of the handle. Bend the paint roller into shape. If desired, Rnds 26—33 of the handle may be sewn to Rnds 13—20 of the roller cover for reinforcement.

BUCKET GRID

Materials

- » #2 fine weight cotton yarn; shown in Woll Butt Camilla, 100% cotton, 138 yd/125 m per 1.75 oz/50 g skein, in colors/amounts as follows:
  - » White, approx 27.6 yd/25 m, 0.35 oz/10 g
  - » Royal Blue, approx 15.8 yd/12.5 m, 0.2 oz/5 g
- » Crochet hook, 2.5 mm
- » Tapestry needle

Instructions

Bucket Grid

Work starts in back-and-forth rows with turning. End every row with ch1; then turn work.

In White, crochet a chain of 16.

Row 1: Work 1 sc in the 2nd ch from the hook, 1 sc in every following ch. (15 sts)
Rows 2–21: 1 sc in every st of the prev row (15 sts). After having completed the last row, don't turn work.
Change to Royal Blue. Crochet an edging around the whole piece, working 1 rnd of sc: Start with ch1, 20 sc at each of the 2 sides, 13 sc at each of the top and bottom edge, and 3 sc into each of the 4 corner sts; join into the rnd with a sl-st into the first stitch. (78 sts)

Break the yarn, leaving a very long tail (at least 79 in/2m), and embroider a grid pattern onto the tray in backstitch, as shown in the photo.

Feet (make 2)

Rnd 1: In Royal Blue, work 4 sc into an adjustable magic ring. (4 sts)
Rnds 2–5: 1 sc in every st of the prev rnd. (4 sts)
Break the yarn, leaving a long tail.

Handles (make 2)

In Royal Blue, crochet a chain of 21.

Row 1: Work 1 sc in the 2nd ch from the hook, 1 sc in each of next 2 chains, 3 sc in next ch, 1 sc in each of next 12 chains, 3 sc in next ch, 1 sc in each of the last 3 chains. (24 sts)
Break the yarn, leaving a long tail.

Finishing

- » Place the 2 handle pieces atop each other, wrong sides facing, and sew them together in overcast stitch. Now, using mattress stitch, sew the 2 feet to the 2 upper corners on the underside of the grid to Rnd 22; then attach the handle to the middle of the top-side of the grid.

BUCKET

Materials

- » #2 fine weight cotton yarn; shown in Woll Butt Camilla, 100% cotton, 138 yd/125 m per 1.75 oz/50 g skein, in colors/amounts as follows:
  - » Emerald, approx 55.2 yd/50 m, 0.7 oz/20 g
  - » Grey, remnant
- » Crochet hook, 2.5 mm
- » Tapestry needle

Instructions

Bucket

Work in rnds. At the beginning of every rnd, ch1; at the end of every rnd, join with a sl-st into the first stitch of the rnd. Do not turn work.

Rnd 1: In Emerald, work 6 sc into an adjustable magic ring. (6 sts)
Rnd 2: [Inc 1] 6 times. (12 sts)
Rnd 3: [1 sc, inc 1] 6 times. (18 sts)
Rnd 4: [2 sc, inc 1] 6 times. (24 sts)
Rnd 5: [3 sc, inc 1] 6 times. (30 sts)
Rnd 6: [4 sc, inc 1] 6 times. (36 sts)
Rnd 7: Working into the back loop of the stitch only, 1 sc in every st of the prev rnd. (36 sts)
Rnd 8: 1 sc in every st of the prev rnd. (36 sts)
Rnd 9: [11 sc, inc 1] 3 times. (39 sts)
Rnds 10–11: 1 sc in every st of the prev rnd. (39 sts)

Rnd 12: [12 sc, inc 1] 3 times. (42 sts)
Rnds 13–14: 1 sc in every st of the prev rnd. (42 sts)
Rnd 15: [13 sc, inc 1] 3 times. (45 sts)
Rnds 16–17: 1 sc in every st of the prev rnd. (45 sts)
Rnd 18: [14 sc, inc 1] 3 times. (48 sts)
Rnds 19–25: 1 sc in every st of the prev rnd. (48 sts)
Break the yarn, leaving a long tail.

Handle

In Grey, crochet a chain of 41.
Row 1: Work 1 sc in the 2nd ch from the hook, 1 sc in every following ch. (40 sts)
Break the working yarn, leaving a long tail.

Finishing

- » Fold Rnds 23–25 of the bucket over to the outside, and sew this rim to the level of Rnd 20, working in basting stitch. Then, sew the handle in backstitch to 2 opposite spots on the outside of the bucket at the level of Rnds 24–25.

AT THE Beauty Salon

"A sparkling evening makeup, please!" After cleansing and nourishing, blush will be applied with a cosmetics brush. Which eye shadow would you prefer? There are plenty of colors to choose from. As a finishing touch, you can get lipstick matching the shade of your nail polish.

LIPSTICK

Materials

» #2 fine weight cotton yarn; shown in Woll Butt Camilla, 100% cotton, 138 yd/125 m per 1.75 oz/50 g skein, in colors/amounts as follows:
  » Black, approx 15.8 yd/12.5 m, 0.2 oz/5 g
  » Pink (or Red), approx 15.8 yd/12.5 m, 0.2 oz/5 g
  » Grey, remnant
» Crochet hook, 2.5 mm
» Polyester fiberfill
» Tapestry needle

Instructions

Work in rnds. At the beginning of every rnd, ch1; at the end of every rnd, join with a sl-st into the first stitch of the rnd. Do not turn work.

Lipstick Tube Base

Rnd 1: In Black, work 6 sc into an adjustable magic ring. (6 sts)
Rnd 2: [Inc 1] 6 times. (12 sts)
Rnd 3: Working into the back loop of the stitch only, 1 sc in every st of the prev rnd. (12 sts)
Rnds 4–10: 1 sc in every st of the prev rnd. (12 sts)
Change to Grey.
Rnd 11: Working into the back loop of the stitch only, 1 sc in every st of the prev rnd. (12 sts)

Rnd 12: 1 sc in every st of the prev rnd. (12 sts)
Stuff with fiberfill.
Rnd 13: [2 sc, dec 1] 3 times. (9 sts)
Change to Pink (or Red).
Rnd 14: Working into the back loop of the stitch only, 1 sc in every st of the prev rnd. (9 sts)
Rnds 15–18: 1 sc in every st of the prev rnd. (9 sts)
Stuff the remaining part with fiberfill, too.
Rnd 19: [1 sc, dec 1] 3 times. (6 sts)
Rnd 20: [Dec 1] 3 times. (3 sts)
Break the working yarn, and thread it with a tapestry needle through all 3 sts. Cinch to close the opening. Secure the yarn to finish off, and hide the end on the inside of the crocheted piece.

Lipstick Tube Cover

Rnd 1: In Black, work 6 sc into an adjustable magic ring. (6 sts)
Rnd 2: [Inc 1] 6 times. (12 sts)
Rnd 3: Working into the back loop of the stitch only, 1 sc in every st of the prev rnd. (12 sts)
Rnds 4–11: 1 sc in every st of the prev rnd. (12 sts)

Finishing

» Break the working yarn, secure and hide the end on the inside. Widen the cover slightly, using your fingers, and then put the cover on the lipstick base.

NAIL POLISH

Materials

» #2 fine weight cotton yarn; shown in Woll Butt Camilla, 100% cotton, 138 yd/125 m per 1.75 oz/50 g skein, in colors/amounts as follows:
  » Purple or Pink, approx 15.8 yd/12.5 m, 0.2 oz/5 g
  » Grey, remnant
» Crochet hook, 2.5 mm
» Polyester fiberfill
» Tapestry needle

Instructions

Work in rnds. At the beginning of every rnd, ch1; at the end of every rnd, join with a sl-st into the first stitch of the rnd. Do not turn work.

Rnd 1: In Purple (or Pink), work 6 sc into an adjustable magic ring. (6 sts)
Rnd 2: [Inc 1] 6 times. (12 sts)
Rnd 3: [1 sc, inc 1] 6 times. (18 sts)
Rnd 4: Working into the back loop of the stitch only, 1 sc in every st of the prev rnd. (18 sts)

Rnds 5—12: 1 sc in every st of the prev rnd. (18 sts)
Stuff the nail polish bottle with fiberfill.
Rnd 13: Working into the back loop of the stitch only, [dec 1] 9 times. (9 sts)
Change to Grey.
Rnds 14—20: 1 sc in every st of the prev rnd. (9 sts)

Finishing

» Stuff the cap of the nail polish bottle with fiberfill, too. Break the working yarn, and thread it with a tapestry needle through all 9 sts. Cinch to close the opening. Secure the yarn to finish off, and hide the end on the inside of the bottle.

WASHCLOTH

Materials

» #2 fine weight cotton yarn; shown in Woll Butt Camilla, 100% cotton, 138 yd/125 m per 1.75 oz/50 g skein, in colors/amounts as follows:
  » Turquoise, approx 55.2 yd/50 m, 0.7 oz/20 g
» Crochet hooks, 3.0 mm and 2.5 mm
» Tapestry needle

Instructions

Work in rnds. Ch1 at the beginning of Rnd 2, and ch3 at the beginning of every following rnd. End every rnd by joining with a sl-st into the first stitch of the rnd. Do not turn work.

In Turquoise and using 3.0 mm hook, crochet a chain of 40, and join into the round with a sl-st into the first chain (40 sts), making sure that the chain is not twisted.

Rnd 1: 1 sc in every ch. (40 sts)

Rnds 2–12: 1 dc in every st of the prev rnd. (40 sts)

Finishing

» Break the yarn, leaving a long tail, and close the opening by sewing the sts together 1 to 1, always inserting the needle into the outer loops of the sts only. Secure the yarn to finish off, and hide the end on the inside.

» For the hanging loop, attach new working yarn with 2.5 mm hook to Rnd 1 at the level of the sl-st, and ch20. Break the working yarn, and sew on the crocheted chain in the same spot it emerged from in overcast stitch.

COMPACT

Materials

Compact

» #2 fine weight cotton yarn; shown in Woll Butt Camilla, 100% cotton, 138 yd/125 m per 1.75 oz/50 g skein, in colors/ amounts as follows:
  » Black, approx 39.4 yd/37.5 m, 0.5 oz/15 g
  » Remnants of Red, Dusty Pink, Turquoise, White, Grey, Lavender, Purple, Pink, Caramel, Yellow, and Royal Blue

Applicator

» #2 fine weight cotton yarn; shown in Woll Butt Camilla, 100% cotton, 138 yd/125 m per 1.75 oz/50 g skein, in colors/ amounts as follows:
  » Emerald, approx 15.8 yd/12.5 m, 0.2 oz/5 g
  » White, remnant
» Polyester fiberfill

For Both

» Crochet hook, 2.5 mm
» Tapestry needle

Instructions

COMPACT

Palette

Work starts in back-and-forth rows with turning. End every row with ch1; then turn work.

In Black, crochet a chain of 26.

Row 1: Work 1 sc in the 2nd ch from the hook, 1 sc in every following ch. (25 sts)
Rows 2–16: 1 sc in every st of the prev row (25 sts). After having completed the last row, don't turn work. Crochet an edging around the whole piece, working 1 rnd of sc: Start with ch1, crochet 15 sc at each of the 2 sides, 23 sc at each of the top and bottom, and 3 sc into each of the 4 corner sts; join into the rnd with a sl-st into the first stitch (88 sts). Break the working yarn, and secure the end.

Blush

Work in rnds. At the beginning of every rnd, ch1; at the end of every rnd, join with a sl-st into the first stitch of the rnd. Do not turn work.

Rnd 1: In Red, work 6 sc into an adjustable magic ring. (6 sts)
Rnd 2: [Inc 1] 6 times. (12 sts)
Rnd 3: [1 sc, inc 1] 6 times. (18 sts)
Rnd 4: [2 sc, inc 1] 6 times. (24 sts)
Break the yarn, leaving a long tail.
Following the same instructions, make another cake of blush in Dusty Pink.

Eye Shadow

Work in rnds. At the beginning of every rnd, ch1; at the end of every rnd, join with a sl-st into the first stitch of the rnd. Do not turn work.

Rnd 1: In Pink, work 6 sc into an adjustable magic ring. (6 sts)
Rnd 2: [Inc 1] 6 times. (12 sts)
Break the yarn, leaving a long tail.
Following the same instructions, make 8 more eye shadows, 1 each in Turquoise, White, Grey, Lavender, Purple, Caramel, Yellow, and Royal Blue.

Finishing

» Working in basting stitch, sew the 9 eye shadow and 2 blush cakes onto the compact case evenly distributed.

EYE SHADOW APPLICATOR

Work in rnds. At the beginning of every rnd, ch1; at the end of every rnd, join with a sl-st into the first stitch of the rnd. Do not turn work.

Rnd 1: In White, work 4 sc into an adjustable magic ring. (4 sts)
Rnd 2: [Inc 1] 4 times. (8 sts)
Rnds 3–4: 1 sc in every st of the prev rnd. (8 sts)
Rnd 5: 1 sc, dec 1, 2 sc, dec 1, 1 sc. (6 sts)
Change to Emerald.
Rnd 6–15: 1 sc in every st of the prev rnd. (6 sts)
Stuff the handle only slightly with fiberfill.

Finishing

» Break the working yarn, thread through all 6 sts with a tapestry needle, and cinch the opening closed. Secure the yarn, and carefully weave in the ends on the inside.

MAKEUP BRUSH

Materials

» #2 fine weight cotton yarn; shown in Woll Butt Camilla, 100% cotton, 138 yd/125 m per 1.75 oz/50 g skein, in colors/amounts as follows:
  » Emerald, approx 15.8 yd/12.5 m, 0.2 oz/5 g
» Eyelash yarn, #4 medium weight; shown in Schachenmayr Brazilia, 100% polyester, 99 yd/90 m per 1.75 oz/50 g skein, in colors/amounts as follows:
  » Black, approx 11.3 yd/9 m, 0.2 oz/5 g (or Woll Butt Camilla)
» Crochet hook, 2.5 mm
» Polyester fiberfill
» Tapestry needle

Instructions

Work in rnds. At the beginning of every rnd, ch1; at the end of every rnd, join with a sl-st into the first stitch of the rnd. Do not turn work.

Rnd 1: In Emerald, work 6 sc into an adjustable magic ring. (6 sts)
Rnd 2: [Inc 1] 6 times. (12 sts)
Rnd 3: Working into the back loop of the stitch only, 1 sc in every st of the prev rnd. (12 sts)
Rnds 4–20: 1 sc in every st of the prev rnd. (12 sts)
Stuff with fiberfill.

Rnd 21: [2 sc, dec 1] 3 times. (9 sts)
Rnd 22: [1 sc, dec 1] 3 times. (6 sts)
Break the working yarn and, using a tapestry needle, thread through all 6 sts. Cinch to close the opening, finish off by securing the yarn, and hide the end on the inside of the brush.

Finishing

» Embroider bristles in eyelash yarn (Schachenmayr Brazilia) in Black with a tapestry needle over the sts of Rnds 1–2, working in basting stitch. Do not pull the strands of yarn taut, but place them over a finger or pen to form loops. As an alternative, you can knot approx. 1.2 in/3 cm long strands of cotton yarn (Woll Butt Camilla) onto Rnds 1–2, and then unply the unattached ends for a frayed look.

CREAM JAR

Materials

» #2 fine weight cotton yarn; shown in Woll Butt Camilla, 100% cotton, 138 yd/125 m per 1.75 oz/50 g skein, in colors/amounts as follows:
  » White, approx 15.8 yd/12.5 m, 0.2 oz/5 g
  » Pink, approx 15.8 yd/12.5 m, 0.2 oz/5 g
  » Dusty Pink, remnant
» Crochet hook, 2.5 mm
» Polyester fiberfill
» Tapestry needle

Instructions

Work in rnds. At the beginning of every rnd, ch1; at the end of every rnd, join with a sl-st into the first stitch of the rnd. Do not turn work.

Jar

Rnd 1: In White, work 6 sc into an adjustable magic ring. (6 sts)
Rnd 2: [Inc 1] 6 times. (12 sts)
Rnd 3: [1 sc, inc 1] 6 times. (18 sts)
Rnd 4: [2 sc, inc 1] 6 times. (24 sts)
Rnd 5: [3 sc, inc 1] 6 times. (30 sts)
Rnd 6: [4 sc, inc 1] 6 times. (36 sts)
Rnd 7: Working into the back loop of the sts only, 1 sc in every st of the prev rnd. (36 sts)
Rnd 8: 1 sc in every st of the prev rnd. (36 sts)
Change to Pink.

Rnds 9–11: 1 sc in every st of the prev rnd. (36 sts)
Change to White.
Rnds 12–13: 1 sc in every st of the prev rnd. (36 sts)
Rnd 14: Working into the back loop of the sts only, [4 sc, dec 1] 6 times. (30 sts)
Rnd 15a: Working into the front loop of the sts only, 1 sc in every st of the prev rnd. (30 sts)
Break the working yarn.

Join new working yarn in Dusty Pink to Rnd 14, and work into the inner, unused loops of the sts as follows:
Rnd 15b: Working into the back loop of the sts only, [3 sc, dec 1] 6 times. (24 sts)
Rnd 16: [2 sc, dec 1] 6 times. (18 sts)

Rnd 17: [1 sc, dec 1] 6 times. (12 sts)
Stuff the piece with fiberfill, and shape it.
Rnd 18: [Dec 1] 6 times. (6 sts)
Break the working yarn, thread through all 6 sts with a tapestry needle, and cinch the opening closed.

Lid

Work the lid in Pink, following instructions for Rnds 1–8 of the jar.

Finishing

» Finish off by securing the yarn, and carefully weave in ends.

TISSUE BOX

Materials

Tissue Box

» #2 fine weight cotton yarn; shown in Woll Butt Camilla, 100% cotton, 138 yd/125 m per 1.75 oz/50 g skein, in colors/amounts as follows:
  » Purple, approx 27.6 yd/25 m, 0.35 oz/ 10 g
  » Lavender, approx 27.6 yd/25 m, 0.35 oz/ 10 g
  » White, approx 15.8 yd/12.5 m, 0.2 oz/5 g
» #2 fine weight cotton yarn; shown in Schachenmayr Catania, 100% cotton, 138 yd/125 m per 1.75 oz/50 g skein, in colors/ amounts as follows:
  » Violet, approx 15.8 yd/12.5 m, 0.2 oz/5 g

Facial Tissues

» #2 fine weight cotton yarn; shown in Woll Butt Camilla, 100% cotton, 138 yd/125 m per 1.75 oz/50 g skein, in colors/amounts as follows:
  » White, approx. 7.9 yd/7.5 m, 0.1 oz/3 g

For Both

» Crochet hook, 2.5 mm
» Tapestry needle

Instructions

TISSUE BOX

Work starts in back-and-forth rows with turning. End every row with ch1; then turn work.

In Purple, crochet a chain of 26.

Row 1: Work 1 sc in the 2nd ch from the hook, 1 sc in every following ch. (25 sts)
Rows 2–12: 1 sc in every st of the prev row (25 sts). After having completed the last row, don't turn work.
Continue as follows, working in rnds: At the beginning of every rnd, ch1; at the end of every rnd, join with a sl-st into the first stitch of the rnd. Do not turn work.
Rnd 13: Crochet an edging around the whole piece, working 80 sc total, of these 11 sc at each of the 2 sides, 23 sc at each of the top and bottom, and 3 sc into each of the 4 corner sts. (80 sts)

Rnd 14: Working into the back loop of the stitch only, 1 sc in every st of the prev rnd. (80 sts)
Rnd 15: 1 sc in every st of the prev rnd. (80 sts) Change to White.
Rnd 16: 1 sc in every st of the prev rnd. (80 sts) Change to Violet.
Rnds 17–18: 1 sc in every st of the prev rnd. (80 sts)
Change to White.
Rnd 19: 1 sc in every st of the prev rnd. (80 sts) Change to Lavender.
Rnds 20–21: 1 sc in every st of the prev rnd. (80 sts)
Change to White.
Rnd 22: 1 sc in every st of the prev rnd. (80 sts) Change to Lavender.
Rnd 23: Working into the back loop of the stitch only, 11 sc, sc3tog (2 sts dec'd), 23 sc, sc3tog (2 sts dec'd), 11 sc, sc3tog (2 sts dec'd), 23 sc, sc3tog (2 sts dec'd) (72 sts). After having finished this rnd, ch1 and turn work.

From here on, work again in back-and-forth rows with turning. End every row with ch1; then turn work.

Rnd 24: Work 1 sc in each of next 24 sts. (24 sts)
Rnds 25–28: 1 sc in every st of the prev row. (24 sts)
Rnd 29: 6 sc, ch12, skip 12 sts, 6 sc. (24 sts)
Rnd 30: 6 sc, 12 sc in ch-sp of the prev row, 6 sc. (24 sts)
Rnds 31–35: 1 sc in every st of the prev row. (24 sts)
Break the yarn, leaving a long tail.

Finishing

» Sew Rnd 23 to Rows 24–35 in overcast stitch. For ease of work, mark the corners with a stitch marker before you start. Finish off by securing the yarn, and weave in the tail.

COTTON PADS

Materials

» #2 fine weight cotton yarn; shown in Woll Butt Camilla, 100% cotton, 138 yd/125 m per 1.75 oz/ 50 g skein, in colors/amounts as follows:
  » White, approx 3.2 yd/2.5 m, 0.04 oz/1 g
» Crochet hook, 2.5 mm
» Tapestry needle

Tip

Fill the tissue box with crocheted tissues, or or use it to store nail polish and lipstick.

FACIAL TISSUES

Work in back-and-forth rows with turning. End every row with ch3; then turn work. In White, crochet a chain of 18.

Row 1: Work 1 dc in the 4th ch from the hook, 1 dc in every following ch. (15 sts)

Rows 2–5: 1 dc in every st of the prev row (15 sts). After having completed the last row, don't turn work. Crochet an edging around the whole tissue, working 1 rnd of sc, starting with ch1 and working 3 sc into each of the 4 corner sts, and join the rnd with 1 sl-st into the first st.

Finishing

» Break the working yarn, secure the end, and weave it in under the sts.

» Following the same instructions, crochet as many tissues as desired, and place them into the tissue box.

Instructions

Work in rnds. At the beginning of every rnd, ch1; at the end of every rnd, join with a sl-st into the first stitch of the rnd. Do not turn work.

Rnd 1: In White, work 6 sc into an adjustable magic ring. (6 sts)

Rnd 2: [Inc 1] 6 times. (12 sts)

Rnd 3: [1 sc, inc 1] 6 times. (18 sts)

Rnd 4: [2 sc, inc 1] 6 times. (24 sts)

Rnd 5: [3 sc, inc 1] 6 times. (30 sts)

Finishing

» Break the working yarn, secure the end, and weave it in under the sts.

» Following the same instructions, make as many cotton pads as desired.

FOR LITTLE
carpenters

Help the young builders go about measuring
with folding ruler and bubble level, sawing,
hammering, and fastening with screws,
until they've remodeled the whole house.

HAMMER AND NAIL

Materials

Hammer

» #2 fine weight cotton yarn; shown in Woll Butt Camilla, 100% cotton, 138 yd/125 m per 1.75 oz/50 g skein, in colors/amounts as follows:
  » Red, approx 27.6 yd/25 m, 0.35 oz/10 g
  » Black, approx 27.6 yd/25 m, 0.35 oz/10 g
» Polyester fiberfill

Nail

» #2 fine weight cotton yarn; shown in Woll Butt Camilla, 100% cotton, 138 yd/125 m per 1.75 oz/50 g skein, in colors/amounts as follows:
  » Grey, approx 15.8 yd/12.5 m, 0.2 oz/5 g

For Both

» Crochet hook, 2.5 mm
» Tapestry needle

Instructions

HAMMER

Hammer Handle

Work in rnds. At the beginning of every rnd, ch1; at the end of every rnd, join with a sl-st into the first stitch of the rnd. Do not turn work.

Rnd 1: In Red, work 6 sc into an adjustable magic ring. (6 sts)
Rnd 2: [Inc 1] 6 times. (12 sts)
Rnds 3–20: 1 sc in every st of the prev rnd. (12 sts)
Break the working yarn, leaving a long tail, and stuff the handle with fiberfill.

Hammer Head

Work starts in back-and-forth rows with turning. End every row with ch1; then turn work.

In Black, crochet a chain of 6.

Row 1: Work 1 sc in the 2nd ch from the hook, 1 sc in every following ch. (5 sts)
Rows 2–5: 1 sc in every st of the prev row (5 sts). After having completed the last row, don't turn work.
Continue as follows, working in rnds: Begin every rnd with ch1, end every rnd with 1 sl-st into the first st. Do not turn work.
Rnd 6: Crochet an edging around the whole piece, working 26 sc total, of these, 4 sc at each of the 2 sides, 3 sc at each of the top and bottom, and 3 sc into each of the 4 corner sts. (26 sts)
Rnd 7: Working into the back loop of the stitch only, 1 sc in every st of the prev rnd. (26 sts)
Rnds 8–16: 1 sc in every st of the prev rnd. (26 sts)
Rnd 17: 4 sc, dec 1, 11 sc, dec 1, 7 sc. (24 sts)
Rnd 18: 3 sc, dec 1, 10 sc, dec 1, 7 sc. (22 sts)
Rnd 19: 3 sc, dec 1, 9 sc, dec 1, 6 sc. (20 sts)

Rnd 20: 2 sc, dec 1, 9 sc, dec 1, 5 sc. (18 sts)
Rnd 21: 2 sc, dec 1, 8 sc, dec 1, 4 sc. (16 sts)
Rnd 22: 1 sc, dec 1, 7 sc, dec 1, 4 sc. (14 sts)
Rnd 23: 1 sc, dec 1, 6 sc, dec 1, 3 sc. (12 sts)
Rnd 24: 1 sc, dec 1, 5 sc, dec 1, 2 sc. (10 sts)
Break the working yarn, leaving a long tail. Now, stuff the hammer head with fiberfill, and shape it. Close the sts of the remaining opening with a tapestry needle 1 to 1 in overcast stitch, inserting the needle into the outer loops of the crochet sts only.

Finishing

» Thread the red tail into a tapestry needle, and sew the handle to the sts of Rnds 10–14 of the hammer head in overcast stitch, at the side where the ends of the rounds are located on the hammer head.

SCREWDRIVER

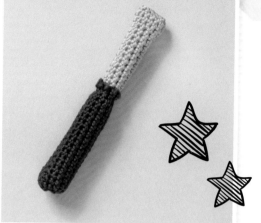

Materials

- » #2 fine weight cotton yarn; shown in Woll Butt Camilla, 100% cotton, 138 yd/125 m per 1.75 oz/50 g skein, in colors/amounts as follows:
  - » Grey, approx 15.8 yd/12.5 m, 0.2 oz/5 g
- » #2 fine weight cotton yarn; shown in Schachenmayr Catania, 100% cotton, 138 yd/125 m per 1.75 oz/50 g skein, in colors/amounts as follows:
  - » Jeans, approx 15.8 yd/12.5 m, 0.2 oz/5 g
- » Crochet hook, 2.5 mm
- » Polyester fiberfill
- » Tapestry needle

NAIL

Work in rnds. At the beginning of every rnd, ch1; at the end of every rnd, join with a sl-st into the first stitch of the rnd. Do not turn work.

Nail Head with Attached Shank

Rnd 1: In Grey, work 4 sc into an adjustable magic ring. (4 sts)
Rnds 2–10: 1 sc in every st of the prev rnd. (4 sts)
Rnd 11: Working into the front loop of the stitch only, [inc 1] 4 times. (8 sts)
Rnd 12: [1 sc, inc 1] 4 times. (12 sts)
Rnd 13: [2 sc, inc 1] 4 times. (16 sts)
Break the working yarn.

Additional Nail Head (for reinforcement)

Rnd 1: In Grey, work 4 sc into an adjustable magic ring. (4 sts)
Rnd 2: [Inc 1] 4 times. (8 sts)
Rnd 3: [1 sc, inc 1] 4 times. (12 sts)
Rnd 4: [2 sc, inc 1] 4 times. (16 sts)

Finishing

- » Place the additional nail head onto the nail head with attached shank, and sew both pieces together in overcast stitch. Break the working yarn, secure, and weave in the end.

Instructions

Work in rnds. At the beginning of every rnd, ch1; at the end of every rnd, join with a sl-st into the first stitch of the rnd. Do not turn work.

Rnd 1: In Jeans, work 6 sc into an adjustable magic ring. (6 sts)
Rnd 2: [Inc 1] 6 times. (12 sts)
Rnds 3–17: 1 sc in every st of the prev rnd. (12 sts)
Rnd 18: [2 sc, dec 1] 3 times. (9 sts)
Rnd 19: 1 sc in every st of the prev rnd. (9 sts)
Rnd 20a: Working into the front loop of the stitch only, 1 sc in every st of the prev rnd. (9 sts)
Break the working yarn.
Stuff the handle.
Attach new working yarn in Grey to the unused back loop, and continue as follows:
Rnd 20b: Working into the back loop of the stitch only, 1 sc in every st of the prev rnd. (9 sts)
Rnds 21–30: 1 sc in every st of the prev rnd. (9 sts)

Rnd 31: [2 sc, inc 1] 3 times. (12 sts)
Rnd 32: 1 sc in every st of the prev rnd. (12 sts)
Rnd 33: [Dec 1, 4 sc] 2 times. (10 sts)
Stuff the shank of the screwdriver with fiberfill, too. Now, break the working yarn, leaving a long tail, and close the sts of the opening 1 to 1 with a tapestry needle in overcast stitch, inserting the needle in the outer loops of the sts only.

Finishing

- » Secure the yarn, and carefully weave in the ends on the inside.

Tip

Since the color change in Rnd 20 is somewhat tricky to work, it is recommended after Rnd 19 to first work Rnd 20b, then stuff the handle, and work Rnd 20a last.

PLIERS

Materials

» #2 fine weight cotton yarn; shown in Woll Butt Camilla, 100% cotton, 138 yd/125 m per 1.75 oz/50 g skein, in colors/amounts as follows:
  » Kiwi, approx 27.6 yd/25 m, 0.35 oz/10 g
  » Grey, approx 15.8 yd/12.5 m, 0.2 oz/5 g
» Crochet hook, 2.5 mm
» Polyester fiberfill
» Tapestry needle

Instructions

Handles with Blades (make 2)

Work in rnds. At the beginning of every rnd, ch1; at the end of every rnd, join with a sl-st into the first stitch of the rnd. Do not turn work.

Rnd 1: In Kiwi, work 6 sc into an adjustable magic ring. (6 sts)
Rnd 2: [Inc 1] 6 times. (12 sts)
Rnds 3–15: 1 sc in every st of the prev rnd. (12 sts)
Change to Grey.
Rnd 16: Working into the back loop of the stitch only, 1 sc in every st of the prev rnd. (12 sts)
Stuff the handles with fiberfill and nudge them into a rounded shape.

Rnd 17: [Dec 1, 4 sc] 2 times. (10 sts)
Rnds 18–19: 1 sc in every st of the prev rnd. (10 sts)
Rnd 20: [Dec 1, 3 sc] 2 times. (8 sts)
Rnds 21–22: 1 sc in every st of the prev rnd. (8 sts)
Rnd 23: [Dec 1, 2 sc] 2 times. (6 sts)
Rnds 24–25: 1 sc in every st of the prev rnd. (6 sts)
Rnd 26: [Dec 1, 1 sc] 2 times. (4 sts)
Rnds 27–28: 1 sc in every st of the prev rnd. (4 sts)
Break the working yarn, thread it through all 4 sts with a tapestry needle, and cinch the opening closed. Now, finish off, secure the end, and weave it in on the inside. The grey blade tips stay unstuffed.

Finishing

» Place both handles with blades slightly overlapping on the diagonal, and sew them together in basting stitch at the level of Rnd 18 over the width of 1 st.

SAW

Materials

» #2 fine weight cotton yarn; shown in Woll Butt Camilla, 100% cotton, 138 yd/125 m per 1.75 oz/50 g skein, in colors/amounts as follows:
  » Grey, approx 27.6 yd/25 m, 0.35 oz/10 g
» #2 fine weight cotton yarn; shown in Schachenmayr Catania, 100% cotton, 138 yd/125 m per 1.75 oz/50 g skein, in colors/amounts as follows:
  » Sun, approx 15.8 yd/12.5 m, 0.2 oz/5 g
» Crochet hook, 2.5 mm
» Tapestry needle

Instructions

Saw Blade (make 2)

Work in back-and-forth rows with turning. End every row with ch1; then turn work.

In Grey, crochet a chain of 13.
Row 1: Work 1 sc in the 2nd ch from the hook, 1 sc in every following ch. (12 sts)
Row 2: 1 sc into each of the first 10 sts of the prev row, dec 1. (11 sts)
Row 3: Dec 1, 1 sc in each of next 9 sts of the prev row. (10 sts)
Row 4: 1 sc in every st of the prev row, ch3. (13 sts)
Row 5: Without additional turning chain, 1 sc in each of the 2nd and 3rd ch from the hook, 1 sc in every sc of the prev row. (12 sts)
Rows 6–21: Repeat Rows 2–5 four times.
Row 22: 1 sc into each of the first 10 sts of the prev row, dec 1. (11 sts)
Row 23: Dec 1, 1 sc in each of next 9 sts of the prev row. (10 sts)

Row 24: Dec 1, 1 sc in each of next 6 sts of the prev row, dec 1. (8 sts)
Row 25: Dec 1, 1 sc in each of next 4 sts of the prev row, dec 1. (6 sts)
Break the working yarn, leaving a long tail. Place both pieces atop each other, wrong sides facing, and sew together in basting stitch with a tapestry needle, using the long tail.

Handle

Attach new working yarn in Sun to Row 1 of the 2 joined saw blades.

Row 1: 1 sc in every one of the 12 chains; at the end of the row, ch1, and then turn work. (12 sts)
Now, work the next row/rnd as follows:
Rnd 2: Working in back loops only, 1 sc into each of the first 3 sts of the prev row, ch1, turn, and then work 3 sc in the front loops of the same sts, join into the round with 1 sl-st into the first st. (7 sts)

From here on, continue in rnds. At the beginning of every rnd, ch1; at the end of every rnd, join with a sl-st into the first stitch of the rnd. Do not turn work.
Rnd 3: 1 sc in every st of the prev rnd, except for the ch in the middle, which gets skipped. (6 sts)
Rnds 4–25: 1 sc in every st of the prev rnd. (6 sts)
Break the working yarn, leaving a long tail, and use it to sew Rnd 25 to the first 3 sts of Row 1.

Finishing

» Secure all ends, and weave in the tails.

FOLDING RULER

Materials

» #2 fine weight cotton yarn; shown in Woll Butt Camilla, 100% cotton, 138 yd/125 m per 1.75 oz/50 g skein, in colors/amounts as follows:
  » Yellow, approx 39.4 yd/37.5 m, 0.5 oz/15 g
  » Grey, approx 15.8 yd/12.5 m, 0.2 oz/5 g
  » Black, remnant
» Crochet hook, 2.5 mm
» Tapestry needle

Instructions

Rule Strips (make 3)

Work in rnds. At the beginning of every rnd, ch1; at the end of every rnd, join with a sl-st into the first stitch of the rnd. Do not turn work.

In Grey, crochet a chain of 6.

Rnd 1: Work 1 sc in the 2nd ch from the hook, 1 sc in each of next 3 chains, 3 sc in the last ch, and then continue into the unused loops on the other side of the chain, working 1 sc in each of next 3 chains, and 2 sc in the 5th chain. Join the rnd with 1 sl-st into the first stitch. (12 sts)

Rnd 2: 1 sc in every st of the prev rnd. (12 sts) Change to Yellow.

Rnds 3–25: 1 sc in every st of the prev rnd. (12 sts)
Change to Grey.

Rnd 26: 1 sc in every st of the prev rnd. (12 sts)

Rnd 27: Ch1, turn, pat flat, and then [sc2tog opposite sts] 6 times to crochet the 12 sts of the prev rnd together (6 sts). Break the yarn, leaving a long tail.

Finishing

» Embroider evenly spaced gradation marks in Black onto the front and back of the rule strips in running stitch. Always work 4 short lines over 1 st, followed by 1 long line over 3 sts. Begin and end the strip with 1 long line. Now, sew the rule strips together at the short sides in Grey in mattress stitch over the 2 middle sts. Make sure that the gradation marks on all rule strips face in the same direction.

» Finish off, secure the end, and weave in all ends.

WRENCH

Materials

» #2 fine weight cotton yarn; shown in Woll Butt Camilla, 100% cotton, 138 yd/125 m per 1.75 oz/50 g skein, in colors/amounts as follows:
  » Grey, approx 27.6 yd/25 m, 0.35 oz/10 g
» Crochet hook, 2.5 mm
» Tapestry needle

Instructions

Work in rnds. At the beginning of every rnd, ch1; at the end of every rnd, join with a sl-st into the first stitch of the rnd. Only turn work when this is explicitly stated in the instructions!

Rnd 1: In Grey, work 6 sc into an adjustable magic ring. (6 sts)
Rnd 2: [Inc 1] 6 times. (12 sts)
Rnds 3—17: 1 sc in every st of the prev rnd. (12 sts)
Rnd 18: 4 sc, inc 1, 5 sc, inc 1, 1 sc. (14 sts)
Rnd 19: 4 sc, inc 1, 6 sc, inc 1, 2 sc. (16 sts)
Rnd 20: 5 sc, inc 1, 7 sc, inc 1, 2 sc. (18 sts)
Rnds 21—22: 1 sc in every st of the prev rnd. (18 sts)

Rnd 23: Ch1, turn, 1 sc in each of next 6 sts of the prev rnd, join into rnd with a sl-st into the first st. Leave the remaining 12 sts unworked. (6 sts)
Rnd 24: Ch1, turn, 1 sc in every st of the prev rnd. (6 sts)
Rnd 25: 1 sc in every st of the prev rnd. (6 sts)
Rnd 26: 2 sc, dec 1, 2 sc. (5 sts)
Rnd 27: 1 sc, dec 1, 2 sc. (4 sts)
Break the working yarn, thread it through all 4 sts with a tapestry needle, and cinch the opening closed. Secure the end, and weave it in on the inside. Attach new working yarn at the 7th st of Rnd 22.

Crochet opposite sts together with a sl-st as follows: 7th with 18th st, 8th with 17th st, 9th with 16th st. For the last 6 unused sts (10th—15th sts), repeat Rnds 23—27, but without turning work.
Break the working yarn, thread it through all 4 sts with a tapestry needle, and cinch the opening closed.

Finishing

» Secure the yarn, and hide the end neatly on the inside of the wrench.

BUBBLE LEVEL

Materials

» #2 fine weight cotton yarn; shown in Schachenmayr Catania, 100% cotton, 138 yd/125 m per 1.75 oz/50 g skein, in colors/amounts as follows:
  » Sun, approx 86.7 yd/75 m, 1.1 oz/30 g
» #2 fine weight cotton yarn; shown in Woll Butt Camilla, 100% cotton, 138 yd/125 m per 1.75 oz/50 g skein, in colors/amounts as follows:
  » Red, approx 15.8 yd/12.5 m, 0.2 oz/5 g

» Black, approx 15.8 yd/12.5 m, 0.2 oz/5 g
» Light Green, approx 15.8 yd/12.5 m, 0.2 oz/5 g
» White, approx 15.8 yd/12.5 m, 0.2 oz/5 g
» Crochet hook, 2.5 mm
» Polyester fiberfill
» Tapestry needle

Level Housing

Work starts in back-and-forth rows with turning. End every row with ch1; then turn work.

In Red, crochet a chain of 8.

Row 1: Work 1 sc in the 2nd ch from the hook, 1 sc in every following ch. (7 sts)
Row 2: 1 sc in every st of the prev row. (7 sts) Do not turn work at the end of this row! Continue as follows, working in rnds: At the beginning of every rnd, ch1; at the end of every rnd, join with a sl-st into the first stitch of the rnd. Do not turn work.
Rnd 3: Crochet an edging around the whole piece, working 24 sc total, of these 1 sc at each of the 2 narrow sides, 5 sc at each of the long sides, and 3 sc into each of the 4 corner sts. (24 sts)
Rnd 4: Working into the back loop of the stitch only, 1 sc in every st of the prev rnd. (24 sts) Change to Sun.
Rnd 5: Working into the back loop of the stitch only, 1 sc in every st of the prev rnd. (24 sts)
Rnds 6–45: 1 sc in every st of the prev rnd. (24 sts)
Change to Red.
Rnd 46: Working into the front loop of the stitch only, 1 sc in every st of the prev rnd. (24 sts) After having completed the last rnd, ch1, and turn work.
From here on, continue in rows. End every row with ch1; then turn work.
Row 47: Working into the front loop of the stitch only, 1 sc in each of next 7 sts. (7 sts)
Rows 48–50: 1 sc in every st of the prev row. (7 sts)
Break the working yarn, leaving a long tail. Now, stuff the level housing with fiberfill, and

shape it. Then, sew Rows 47–50 to Rnd 46 in overcast stitch. Secure the yarn, and hide the end on the inside.

Round Bubble Window (make 2)

Work in rnds. At the beginning of every rnd, ch1; at the end of every rnd, join with a sl-st into the first stitch of the rnd. Do not turn work.
Rnd 1: In White, work 6 sc into an adjustable magic ring. (6 sts)
Rnd 2: [Inc 1] 6 times. (12 sts)
Rnd 3: [1 sc, inc 1] 6 times. (18 sts)
Change to Black.
Rnd 4: [2 sc, inc 1] 6 times. (24 sts)
Break the yarn, leaving a long tail.

Elongated Bubble Tube (make 2)

In Light Green, crochet a chain of 6.
Rnd 1: Work 1 sc in the 2nd ch from the hook, 1 sc in each of next 3 chains, 3 sc in the last ch, and then continue into the unused loops on the other side of the chain, working 1 sc in each of next 3 chains, 2 sc in the 5th ch, join into rnd with a sl-st into the first stitch. (12 sts)
Break the yarn, leaving a long tail.

Square Bubble Window

Work starts in back-and-forth rows with turning. End every row with ch1; then turn work.
In Light Green, crochet a chain of 8.
Row 1: Work 1 sc in the 2nd ch from the hook, 1 sc in every following ch. (7 sts)
Rows 2–7: 1 sc in every st of the prev row (7 sts). After having completed the last row, don't turn work.
Continue as follows, working in rnds: At the beginning of every rnd, ch1 and join into rnd with a sl-st into the first stitch. Do not turn work.

Rnd 8: Crochet an edging around the whole piece, working 34 sc total, of these 6 sc at each of the 2 sides, 5 sc at each of the top and bottom, and 3 sc into each of the 4 corner sts. (34 sts)
Change to White.
Rnd 9: Work 1 sc in each of next 7 sts of the prev rnd, 3 sc in the next st (2 sts inc'd), 1 sc in each of next 7 sts of the prev rnd, 3 sc in the next st, 1 sc in each of next 8 sts of the prev rnd, 3 sc in the next st, 1 sc in each of next 7 sts of the prev rnd, 3 sc in the next st, 1 sc in the next st. (42 sts)
Change to Black.
Rnd 10: 1 sc in each of the next 8 sts of the prev rnd, 3 sc in the next st, 1 sc in each of next 9 sts of the prev rnd, 3 sc in the next st, 1 sc in each of next 10 sts of the prev rnd, 3 sc in the next st, 1 sc in each of next 9 sts of the prev rnd, 3 sc in the next st, 1 sc in each of next 2 sts. (50 sts)
Break the working yarn, leaving a long tail.

Finishing

» Place 1 bubble tube atop the middle of a round bubble window, and sew it on in basting stitch. In Black, embroider 2 gradation marks onto the bubble window in backstitch. Now, sew the 2 round bubble windows to the 2 broad sides of the level housing in basting stitch at the level of Rnds 7–14. Embroider the square bubble window, too, in backstitch with 2 gradation marks in Black, placed in Rows 2 and 6. Sew the assembled embellishment onto the level housing in basting stitch, placing it centered over a side edge at the level of Rnds 21–32.

» Secure all ends, and hide them on the inside.

SCREW

Materials

- » #2 fine weight cotton yarn; shown in Woll Butt Camilla, 100% cotton, 138 yd/125 m per 1.75 oz/50 g skein, in colors/amounts as follows:
  - » Grey, approx 15.8 yd/12.5 m, 0.2 oz/5 g
- » Crochet hook, 2.5 mm
- » Polyester fiberfill
- » Tapestry needle

Instructions

Work in rnds. At the beginning of every rnd, ch1; at the end of every rnd, join with a sl-st into the first stitch of the rnd. Do not turn work.

Rnd 1: In Grey, work 6 sc into an adjustable magic ring. (6 sts)
Rnd 2: [Inc 1] 6 times. (12 sts)
Rnd 3: [1 sc, inc 1] 6 times. (18 sts)
Rnd 4: Working into the back loop of the stitch only, 1 sc in every st of the prev rnd. (18 sts)
Rnd 5: 1 sc in every st of the prev rnd. (18 sts)
Rnd 6: Working into the back loop of the stitch only, [dec 1] 9 times. (9 sts)

Stuff the head of the screw with fiberfill.
Rnd 7: Working into the front loop of the stitch only, 1 sc in every st of the prev rnd. (9 sts)
Rnds 8–13: 1 sc in every st of the prev rnd. (9 sts)
Finish stuffing the remaining space.
Rnd 14: [1 sc, dec 1] 3 times. (6 sts)
Rnd 15: 1 sc in every st of the prev rnd. (6 sts)
Break the working yarn, leaving a long tail, thread it through all 6 sts with a tapestry needle, and cinch the opening closed.

Finishing

- » In Grey, embroider screw threads in backstitch diagonally over Rnds 8–13, and a slot or X over Rnds 1–3. Secure the yarn, and hide the end on the inside.

NUT

Materials

» #2 fine weight cotton yarn; shown in Woll Butt Camilla, 100% cotton, 138 yd/125 m per 1.75 oz/50 g skein, in colors/amounts as follows:
  » Grey, approx 15.8 yd/12.5 m, 0.2 oz/5 g
» Crochet hook, 2.5 mm
» Tapestry needle

Instructions

Work in rnds. At the beginning of every rnd, ch1; at the end of every rnd, join with a sl-st into the first stitch of the rnd. Do not turn work.

Rnd 1: In Grey, crochet a chain of 15, and join into rnd with a sl-st into the first chain. (15 sts)

Rnd 2: Work the following into the chain of 15: [2 sc, inc 1] 5 times. (20 sts)

Rnds 3—5: [3 sc, 1 bpsc] 5 times. (20 sts)

Rnd 6: [2 sc, dec 1] 5 times. (15 sts)

Finishing

» Break the working yarn, leaving a long tail, place Rnds 1 and 6 atop each other, and, in Grey, sew the sts together 1 to 1 in overcast stitch. Secure the yarn, and hide the end on the inside.

IN THE
Garden

Everything is blooming and flourishing because some serious gardening is going on! Seeds are sown and bulbs planted. To make sure everything grows, we are wielding a rake and watering with abundance so we can harvest fresh vegetables soon.

PLANTER

Materials

» #2 fine weight cotton yarn; shown in Woll Butt Camilla, 100% cotton, 138 yd/125 m per 1.75 oz/50 g skein, in colors/amounts as follows:
  » Yellow, approx 71 yd/62.5 m, 0.9 oz/25 g
  » Chocolate, approx 55.2 yd/50 m, 0.7 oz/20 g

» Crochet hook, 3.0 mm
» Polyester fiberfill
» Tapestry needle

Planter

Work starts in back-and-forth rows with turning. End every row with ch1; then turn work.

In Yellow, crochet a chain of 37.

Row 1: Work 1 sc in the 2nd ch from the hook, 1 sc in every following ch. (36 sts)
Rows 2–12: 1 sc in every st of the prev row (36 sts). After having completed the last row, don't turn work.
From here on, continue in the round. At the beginning of every round, ch1, and at the end, join with a sl-st into the first stitch of the rnd. Do not turn work.
Rnd 13: Crochet an edging around the whole piece, working 102 sc total, of these 11 sc at each of the 2 sides, 34 sc at each of the top and bottom, and 3 sc into each of the 4 corner sts. (102 sts)
Rnd 14: Working into the back loop of the sts only, 1 sc in every st of the prev rnd. (102 sts)
Rnds 15–19: Begin every rnd with ch2, and then work 1 hdc in every st of the prev rnd. (102 sts)
Rnd 20: Start rnds again with ch1 only, and work in the front loop of the stitch only, 1 sc in every st of the prev rnd. (102 sts)
Break the working yarn, and secure the end.

Potting Soil (make 3)

Work in rnds. At the beginning of every rnd, ch1; at the end of every rnd, join with a sl-st into the first stitch of the rnd. Do not turn work.

Rnd 1: In Chocolate, work 6 sc into an adjustable magic ring. (6 sts)
Rnd 2: [Inc 1] 6 times. (12 sts)
Rnd 3: [1 sc, inc 1] 6 times. (18 sts)
Rnd 4: [2 sc, inc 1] 6 times. (24 sts)
Rnd 5: [3 sc, inc 1] 6 times. (30 sts)
Rnd 6: Working into the back loop of the sts only, 1 sc in every st of the prev rnd. (30 sts)
Rnds 7–10: 1 sc in every st of the prev row. (30 sts)
Rnd 11: [Inc 1, 14 sc] 2 times. (32 sts)
Rnd 12: Working into the front loop of the sts only, 4 sc, [3 sc in 1 sc (2 sts inc'd), 7 sc] 3 times, 3 sc in 1 st, 3 sc. (40 sts)
Rnd 13: 5 sc, [3 sc in 1 sd, 9 sc] 3 times, 3 sc in 1 sc, 4 sc. (48 sts)
Break the working yarn, leaving a long tail.

Finishing

» Place the 3 pieces of potting soil side by side, and sew adjoining edges together in mattress stitch. Then place the joined potting soil assembly into the planter, and sew it on in overcast stitch along the unused inner loops of the sts from Rnd 20. For better orientation, mark the corners with stitch markers or with a piece of contrasting yarn before you start. Stuff the voids between soil and planter with fiberfill as you go.

» The planter is now ready to be filled with seedlings (see pages 76 and 77 for instructions to make seedlings).

Tip

If using a different yarn or or a different hook size than listed, please make sure that the hook size used for the planter is 0.5 mm larger than the hook size for the seedlings, so that the finished pieces will fit into one another.

SEEDLINGS IN POTTING SOIL

Materials

» #2 fine weight cotton yarn; shown in Woll Butt Camilla, 100% cotton, 138 yd/125 m per 1.75 oz/50 g skein, in colors/amounts as follows:
  » Chocolate, approx 27.6 yd/25 m, 0.35 oz/10 g
  » Remnants in Green, Kiwi, Red, and Orange

» Crochet hook, 2.5 mm
» Polyester fiberfill
» Tapestry needle

Work in rnds. At the beginning of every rnd, ch1; at the end of every rnd, join with a sl-st into the first stitch of the rnd. Do not turn work.

Potting Soil with No Plant

Rnd 1: In Chocolate, work 6 sc into an adjustable magic ring. (6 sts)
Rnd 2: [Inc 1] 6 times. (12 sts)
Rnd 3: [1 sc, inc 1] 6 times. (18 sts)
Rnd 4: [2 sc, inc 1] 6 times. (24 sts)
Rnd 5: [3 sc, inc 1] 6 times. (30 sts)
Rnd 6: Working into the back loop of the sts only, 1 sc in every st of the prev rnd. (30 sts)
Rnds 7–10: 1 sc in every st of the prev rnd. (30 sts)
Rnd 11: [3 sc, dec 1] 6 times. (24 sts)
Rnd 12: [2 sc, dec 1] 6 times. (18 sts)
Rnd 13: [1 sc, dec 1] 6 times. (12 sts)
Stuff with fiberfill.
Rnd 14: [Dec 1] 6 times. (6 sts)
Break the working yarn and, using a tapestry needle, thread through all 6 sts. Cinch to close the opening. Secure the yarn to finish off, and hide the end on the inside of the crocheted piece.

Potting Soil with Lettuce Seedling

Follow instructions for potting soil up to Rnd 14, and then continue as follows:
Change to Kiwi.
Rnd 15: 1 sc in every st of the prev rnd. (6 sts)
From here on, continue in rows, ending every row with ch1; then turn work.
Row 16: Ch1, turn, 1 sc in each of next 3 sts of the prev rnd. (3 sts)
Rows 17–21: 1 sc in every st of the prev row. (3 sts)
Row 22: Dec 1, 1 sc. (2 sts)
Row 23: Dec 1. (1 st)
Break the working yarn, and secure the end.

Attach new working yarn in Kiwi to Rnd 15, leaving a long tail, and rep Rows 16–23 for the 3 unused sts.
Use the long beginning tail to close the opening between the 2 leaves in mattress stitch.
Finish off, secure the ends, and hide them on the inside.

Potting Soil with Flower Bulb Seedling

Follow instructions for potting soil up to Rnd 13. Now, stuff with fiberfill, and continue as follows:
Rnd 14: [2 sc, dec 1] 3 times. (9 sts)
Change to Green.
Rnds 15–20: 1 sc in every st of the prev rnd. (9 sts)
Rnd 21: [1 sc, dec 1] 3 times. (6 sts)
Rnd 22: 1 sc in every st of the prev rnd. (6 sts)
Rnd 23: [Dec 1] 3 times. (3 sts)
Break the working yarn, and thread it with a tapestry needle through all 3 sts. Cinch to close the opening. Secure the yarn to finish off, and hide the end on the inside of the crocheted piece.

Potting Soil with Radish Seedling

Follow instructions for potting soil up to Rnd 13. Now, stuff with fiberfill, and continue as follows:
Change to Red.
Rnd 14: 1 sc in every st of the prev rnd. (12 sts)
Rnd 15: [Dec 1] 6 times. (6 sts)
Change to Green.
From here on, continue in rows, ending every row with ch1; then turn work.
Row 16: Ch1, turn, 1 sc in the next st, sc2tog the next 2 sts of the prev rnd. (2 sts)
Rows 17–18: 1 sc in every st of the prev row. (2 sts)
Row 19: 1 sc in the next st, inc 1 (3 sts). At the end of this row, ch3 for turning; then turn.
Row 20: 2 dc in the 1st sc of the prev row, [1 hdc, 1 sc, 1 hdc] in the 2nd sc of the prev row,

[2 dc, ch3, 1 sl-st] in the 3rd sc of the prev row. Break the working yarn, and secure the end.
Attach new working yarn in Green to Rnd 15, leaving a long beginning tail, and rep Rows 16–20 for the 3 unused sts. Use the long beginning tail to close the opening between the 2 leaves in mattress stitch.
Finish off, secure all ends, and hide them on the inside.

Potting Soil with Carrot Seedling

Follow instructions for potting soil up to Rnd 13. Now, stuff with fiberfill, and continue as follows:
Change to Orange.
Rnds 14–15: 1 sc in every st of the prev rnd. (12 sts)
Add more fiberfill.
Rnd 16: [Dec 1] 6 times. (6 sts)
Change to Green.
Rnd 17: [Ch20, 1 sc in the next st of the prev rnd] 6 times, ending with 1 sl-st in the 1st st. Break the working yarn. Secure the yarn, and weave in all ends.

Finishing

» The seedlings are now ready to be placed into the planter with potting soil (see pages 74 and 75).

CARROT & RADISH

Materials

Carrot

» #2 fine weight cotton yarn; shown in Woll Butt Camilla, 100% cotton, 138 yd/125 m per 1.75 oz/50 g skein, in colors/amounts as follows:
  » Orange, approx 27.6 yd/25 m, 0.35 oz/10 g
  » Green, remnant

Radish

» #2 fine weight cotton yarn; shown in Woll Butt Camilla, 100% cotton, 138 yd/125 m per 1.75 oz/50 g skein, in colors/amounts as follows:
  » Red, approx 15.8 yd/12.5 m, 0.2 oz/5 g
  » Green, approx 15.8 yd/12.5 m, 0.2 oz/5 g
  » White, remnant

For Both

» Crochet hook, 2.5 mm
» Polyester fiberfill
» Tapestry needle

Instructions

CARROT

Work in rnds. At the beginning of every rnd, ch1; at the end of every rnd, join with a sl-st into the first stitch of the rnd. Do not turn work.

Rnd 1: In Orange, work 3 sc into an adjustable magic ring. (3 sts)
Rnd 2: [Inc 1] 3 times. (6 sts)
Rnd 3: 1 sc in every st of the prev rnd. (6 sts)
Rnd 4: [1 sc, inc 1] 3 times. (9 sts)
Rnd 5: 1 sc in every st of the prev rnd. (9 sts)
Rnd 6: [2 sc, inc 1] 3 times. (12 sts)
Rnds 7–20: 1 sc in every st of the prev rnd. (12 sts)
Stuff with fiberfill.
Rnd 21: [Dec 1] 6 times. (6 sts)
Change to Green.
Rnd 22: Work [ch20, 1 sc in the next st of the prev rnd] 6 times, ending with 1 sl-st in the 1st st.

Finishing

» Break the working yarn. Secure the yarn, and weave in all ends on the inside.

Tip

The carrot can be worked in spiral rounds instead.

RADISH

Work starts in the round. At the beginning of every rnd, ch1; at the end of every rnd, join with a sl-st into the first stitch of the rnd. Do not turn work.

Rnd 1: In White, work 4 sc into an adjustable magic ring. (4 sts)
Rnd 2: [Inc 1] 4 times. (8 sts)
Change to Red.
Rnd 3: [1 sc, inc 1] 4 times. (12 sts)
Rnd 4: [1 sc, inc 1] 6 times. (18 sts)
Rnds 5–8: 1 sc in every st of the prev rnd. (18 sts)
Rnd 9: [1 sc, dec 1] 6 times. (12 sts)
Stuff with fiberfill.
Rnd 10: [Dec 1] 6 times. (6 sts)
Change to Green.
From here on, continue in rows. End every row with ch1, and turn work.
Row 11: Ch1, turn, 1 sc in each of next 3 sts of the prev rnd. (3 sts)
Rows 12–16: 1 sc in every st of the prev row (3 sts). At the end of the last row, ch2 for turning.
Row 17: (1 hdc, 1 dc, 1 hdc) in the 1st sc of the prev row, (1 dc, 1 tr, 1 trtr, 1 tr, 1 dc) in the 2nd sc of the prev row, (1 hdc, 1 dc, 1 hdc, ch2, 1 sl-st) in the 3rd sc of the prev row.
Break the working yarn and weave in end.
Leaving a long beginning tail, attach new working yarn before the 3 unused sts in Rnd 10, and repeat Rows 11–17.

ONION

Materials

» #2 fine weight cotton yarn; shown in Woll Butt Camilla, 100% cotton, 138 yd/ 125 m per 1.75 oz/50 g skein, in colors/amounts as follows:
  » Caramel, approx 27.6 yd/25 m, 0.35 oz/10 g
  » Remnants in Green and White
» Crochet hook, 2.5 mm
» Polyester fiberfill
» Tapestry needle

Instructions

Work in rnds. At the beginning of every rnd, ch1; at the end of every rnd, join with a sl-st into the first stitch of the rnd. Do not turn work.

Rnd 1: In Caramel, work 6 sc into an adjustable magic ring. (6 sts)
Rnd 2: [Inc 1] 6 times. (12 sts)
Rnd 3: [1 sc, inc 1] 6 times. (18 sts)
Rnd 4: [2 sc, inc 1] 6 times. (24 sts)
Rnd 5: [3 sc, inc 1] 6 times. (30 sts)
Rnds 6—10: 1 sc in every st of the prev rnd. (30 sts)
Rnd 11: [3 sc, dec 1] 6 times. (24 sts)
Rnd 12: [2 sc, dec 1] 6 times. (18 sts)
Rnd 13: [1 sc, dec 1] 6 times. (12 sts)
Stuff with fiberfill.
Rnd 14: [2 sc, dec 1] 3 times. (9 sts)
Change to Green.
Rnds 15—20: 1 sc in every st of the prev rnd. (9 sts)
Rnd 21: [1 sc, dec 1] 3 times. (6 sts)
Rnd 22: 1 sc in every st of the prev rnd. (6 sts)
Rnd 23: [Dec 1] 3 times. (3 sts)
Break the working yarn, and thread it with a tapestry needle through all 3 sts. Cinch to close the opening. Secure the yarn to finish off, and hide the end on the inside of the crocheted piece.

Finishing

» For the hairs, knot 3 to 4 short strands of white yarn to Rnds 1—2, and unply the unattached ends of the strands for a frayed look.

Finishing

» Using the long green tail, close the remaining opening between the 2 leaves in mattress stitch. Firmly knot the white beginning tail once more, and let it dangle.

WATERING CAN

Materials

» #2 fine weight cotton yarn; shown in Woll Butt Camilla, 100% cotton, 138 yd/125 m per 1.75 oz/50 g skein, in colors/amounts as follows:

» White, approx 27.6 yd/25 m, 0.35 oz/10 g

» Orange, approx 27.6 yd/25 m, 0.35 oz/10 g

» Remnants in Yellow and Black

» Crochet hook, 2.5 mm

» Polyester fiberfill

» Tapestry needle

Watering Can

Work in rnds. At the beginning of every rnd, ch1; at the end of every rnd, join with a sl-st into the first stitch of the rnd. Do not turn work.

In Orange, crochet a chain of 11.
Rnd 1: Work 2 sc in the 2nd ch from the hook, 1 sc in each of the following 8 chains, 3 sc in the last ch. Continue in the unused loops on the other side of the chain: 1 sc in every ch. Join into the rnd with a sl-st into the first st. (22 sts)
Rnd 2: Inc 1, 10 sc, [inc 1] 2 times, 8 sc, inc 1. (26 sts)
Rnd 3: 1 sc, inc 1, 10 sc, inc 1, 1 sc, inc 1, 10 sc, inc 1. (30 sts)
Rnd 4: 1 sc, inc 1, 12 sc, inc 1, 1 sc, inc 1, 12 sc, inc 1. (34 sts)
Rnd 5: Working into the back loop of the stitch only, 1 sc in every st of the prev rnd. (34 sts)
Rnds 6–18: 1 sc in every st of the prev rnd. (34 sts)
Rnd 19: Working into the back loop of the stitch only, 1 sc, [dec 1] 2 times, 12 sc, [dec 1] 2 times, 13 sc. (30 sts)
Break the working yarn, secure, and carefully weave in the end.

Spout

Work starts in the round. At the beginning of every rnd, ch1; at the end of every rnd, join with a sl-st into the first stitch of the rnd. Do not turn work!

Rnd 1: In Yellow, work 6 sc into an adjustable magic ring. (6 sts)
Rnd 2: [Inc 1] 6 times. (12 sts)
Rnd 3: 1 sc in every st of the prev rnd. (12 sts) Change to White.
Rnd 4a: Working into the front loop of the stitch only, [[1 sc, 1 hdc, 1 dc) in the first st of the prev rnd, (1 dc, 1 hdc,1 sc) in the next st of the prev rnd] 6 times. (36 sts)
Rnd 4b: Working into the back loop of the stitch only, 1 sc in every st of the prev rnd. (12 sts)
Rnds 5–14: 1 sc in every st of the prev rnd. (12 sts)
From here on, continue in back-and-forth rows with turning.
Row 15: 1 sc in each of the next 6 sts, 1 sl-st in the next st (7 sts). Turn work, but without working a turning chain!
Row 16: Skip the sl-st of the prev row, and work 1 sl-st in the 1st sc of the prev row, 1 sc ea in next 4 sts, 1 sl-st in the next st. (6 sts)
Break the working yarn, leaving a long tail, and stuff the spout with a small amount of fiberfill. It should only be slightly shaped but not become too heavy.

Handle

Work in rnds. At the beginning of every rnd, ch1; at the end of every rnd, join with a sl-st into the first stitch of the rnd. Do not turn work.

In White, and leaving a long beginning tail, crochet a chain of 9, and join the chain into the round with 1 sl-st into the first chain.
Rnd 1: Work 1 sc in every ch. (9 sts)
Rnds 2–30: 1 sc in every st of the prev rnd. (9 sts)
Break the yarn, leaving a long tail.

Finishing

» For the holes in the sprinkler head, embroider little French knots in Black at the level of Rnds 1–3 on the spout. Now, using the long tail, sew the spout to the front of the watering can in overcast stitch, with Rnd 14 of the spout pointing up, and Row 16 down.

» Press the ends of the handle flat, and sew them to the watering can in overcast stitch at the level of Rnd 19.

SEED PACKET

Materials

- » #2 fine weight cotton yarn; shown in Woll Butt Camilla, 100% cotton, 138 yd/125 m per 1.75 oz/50 g skein, in colors/amounts as follows:
  - » White, approx 27.6 yd/25 m, 0.35 oz/10 g
  - » Remnants in Orange, Red, and Green
- » Crochet hooks, 2.5 mm and 3.0 mm
- » Polyester fiberfill
- » Tapestry needle

Instructions

Seed Packet (make 2)

Always work the first row as row and then continue in rounds. At the beginning of every rnd, ch1; at the end of every rnd, join with a sl-st into the first stitch of the rnd. Do not turn work.

In White and with 3.0 mm hook, crochet a chain of 21.

Row 1: Work 1 sc in the 2nd ch from the hook, 1 sc in every following ch. (20 sts)

Now, join into the round with 1 sl-st into the first sc, and continue in rnds:

Rnds 2–12: 1 sc in every st of the prev rnd. (20 sts)

Row 13: Ch1, turn work, and crochet both sides together with 10 sc.

Break the working yarn, secure, and weave in the end.

Carrot Appliqué

Work in back-and-forth rows with turning. End every row with ch1; then turn work.

In Orange and with 2.5 mm hook, crochet a chain of 2.

Row 1: Work 2 sc into the first ch. (2 sts)

Row 2: 1 sc in every st of the prev row. (2 sts)

Row 3: 1 sc, inc 1. (3 sts)

Rows 4–6: 1 sc in every st of the prev row. (3 sts)

Row 7: 1 sc, dec 1. (2 sts)

Break the working yarn, leaving a long tail.

Radish Appliqué

Work in rnds. At the beginning of every rnd, ch1; at the end of every rnd, join with a sl-st into the first stitch of the rnd. Do not turn work.

Rnd 1: In Red and with 2.5 mm hook, work 6 sc into an adjustable magic ring. (6 sts)

Rnd 2: [Inc 1] 6 times. (12 sts)

Break the working yarn, leaving a long tail.

Finishing

- » Sew 1 appliqué onto each seed packet in basting stitch. For the radish, embroider a root tip in Red in backstitch.

- » Using Green and working in backstitch, now embroider matching leaves for the carrot and the radish onto the seed packet. Finish off, secure the end, and hide all tails on the inside.

PLANTING STICK

Materials

» #2 fine weight cotton yarn; shown in Woll Butt Camilla, 100% cotton, 138 yd/125 m per 1.75 oz/50 g skein, in colors/amounts as follows:
  » Red, approx 27.6 yd/25 m, 0.35 oz/10 g
» Crochet hook, 2.5 mm
» Polyester fiberfill
» Tapestry needle

Instructions

Work in rnds. At the beginning of every rnd, ch1; at the end of every rnd, join with a sl-st into the first stitch of the rnd. Do not turn work.

Planting Stick

Rnd 1: In Red, work 3 sc into an adjustable magic ring. (3 sts)
Rnd 2: [Inc 1] 3 times. (6 sts)
Rnd 3: 1 sc in every st of the prev rnd. (6 sts)
Rnd 4: [1 sc, inc 1] 3 times. (9 sts)
Rnd 5: 1 sc in every st of the prev rnd. (9 sts)
Rnd 6: [2 sc, inc 1] 3 times. (12 sts)
Rnd 7: 1 sc in every st of the prev rnd. (12 sts)
Rnd 8: [3 sc, inc 1] 3 times. (15 sts)
Rnds 9–14: 1 sc in every st of the prev rnd. (15 sts)
Rnd 15: [4 sc, inc 1] 3 times. (18 sts)
Rnds 16–20: 1 sc in every st of the prev rnd. (18 sts)
Stuff with fiberfill.
Rnd 21: [Dec 1] 9 times. (9 sts)
Rnds 22–25: 1 sc in every st of the prev rnd. (9 sts)
Break the working yarn, leaving a long tail, and then stuff the remaining space with fiberfill.

Handle

Rnd 1: In Red, work 6 sc into an adjustable magic ring. (6 sts)
Rnd 2: [Inc 1] 6 times. (12 sts)
Rnds 3–12: 1 sc in every st of the prev rnd. (12 sts)
Stuff with fiberfill.
Rnd 13: [Dec 1] 6 times. (6 sts)
Break the working yarn and, using a tapestry needle, thread through all 6 sts. Cinch to close the opening. Secure the yarn to finish off, and hide the end on the inside of the crocheted piece.

Finishing

» Sew the middle of the handle to the planting stick in overcast stitch at the level of Rnds 6–9. Secure the yarn to finish off, and hide the end on the inside of the planting stick.

HAND RAKE

Materials

- » #2 fine weight cotton yarn; shown in Woll Butt Camilla, 100% cotton, 138 yd/125 m per 1.75 oz/50 g skein, in colors/amounts as follows:
  - » Linen, approx 27.6 yd/25 m, 0.35 oz/10 g
- » #2 fine weight cotton yarn; shown in Schachenmayr Catania, 100% cotton, 138 yd/ 125 m per 1.75 oz/50 g skein, in colors/amounts as follows:
  - » Sun, approx 27.6 yd/25 m, 0.35 oz/10 g
- » Crochet hook, 2.5 mm
- » Polyester fiberfill
- » Tapestry needle

Instructions

Work in rnds. At the beginning of every rnd, ch1; at the end of every rnd, join with a sl-st into the first stitch of the rnd. Do not turn work.

Handle

Rnd 1: In Linen, work 6 sc into an adjustable magic ring. (6 sts)
Rnd 2: [Inc 1] 6 times. (12 sts)
Rnds 3–17: 1 sc in every st of the prev rnd. (12 sts)
Change to Sun.
Rnd 18: Working into the front loop of the stitch only, 1 sc in every st of the prev rnd. (12 sts)
Rnd 19: [Inc 1, 5 sc] 2 times. (14 sts)
Rnd 20: 1 sc, inc 1, 6 sc, inc 1, 5 sc. (16 sts)

Rnd 21: 2 sc, inc 1, 7 sc, inc 1, 5 sc. (18 sts)
Rnd 22: 2 sc, inc 1, 8 sc, inc 1, 6 sc. (20 sts)
Rnd 23: 3 sc, inc 1, 9 sc, inc 1, 6 sc. (22 sts)
Rnd 24: 4 sc, inc 1, 10 sc, inc 1, 6 sc. (24 sts)
Rnds 25–30: 1 sc in every st of the prev rnd. (24 sts)

Break the working yarn, leaving a long tail. Now, stuff the handle with fiberfill, filling only Rnds 1–17, leaving the remaining part empty. Using the long tail and a tapestry needle, sew the sts of the remaining opening together 1 to 1 in overcast stitch, inserting the needle into the outer loops of the crochet sts only. The sts with increases should be at the outside edges of the crocheted piece.

Prongs (make 3)

Rnd 1: In Sun, work 5 sc into an adjustable magic ring. (5 sts)
Rnds 2–7: 1 sc in every st of the prev rnd. (5 sts) Break the working yarn, leaving a long tail.

Finishing

- » Sew the 3 prongs to the handle in overcast stitch at the level of Rnds 29–30. Finish off, secure the end, and hide all tails on the inside.

HAND TROWEL

Materials

» #2 fine weight cotton yarn; shown in Woll Butt Camilla, 100% cotton, 138 yd/125 m per 1.75 oz/50 g skein, in colors/amounts as follows:
  » Linen, approx 27.6 yd/25 m, 0.35 oz/10 g
  » Blue, approx 27.6 yd/25 m, 0.35 oz/10 g
» Crochet hook, 2.5 mm
» Polyester fiberfill
» Tapestry needle

Instructions

Work in rnds. At the beginning of every rnd, ch1; at the end of every rnd, join with a sl-st into the first stitch of the rnd. Do not turn work.

Rnd 1: In Blue, work 6 sc into an adjustable magic ring. (6 sts)
Rnd 2: [Inc 1] 6 times. (12 sts)
Rnd 3: 3 sc, inc 1, 5 sc, inc 1, 2 sc. (14 sts)
Rnd 4: 3 sc, inc 1, 6 sc, inc 1, 3 sc. (16 sts)
Rnd 5: 4 sc, inc 1, 7 sc, inc 1, 3 sc. (18 sts)
Rnd 6: 1 sc in every st of the prev rnd. (18 sts)
Rnd 7: 4 sc, inc 1, 8 sc, inc 1, 4 sc. (20 sts)
Rnds 8–9: 1 sc in every st of the prev rnd. (20 sts)
Rnd 10: 5 sc, inc 1, 9 sc, inc 1, 4 sc. (22 sts)
Rnds 11–12: 1 sc in every st of the prev rnd. (22 sts)
Rnd 13: 5 sc, inc 1, 10 sc, inc 1, 5 sc. (24 sts)
Rnds 14–15: 1 sc in every st of the prev rnd. (24 sts)

Rnd 16: 6 sc, inc 1, 11 sc, inc 1, 5 sc. (26 sts)
Rnds 17–18: 1 sc in every st of the prev rnd. (26 sts)
Rnd 19: 6 sc, inc 1, 12 sc, inc 1, 6 sc. (28 sts)
Rnd 20: 1 sc in every st of the prev rnd. (28 sts) Change to Linen.
Rnd 21: Working into the back loop of the stitch only, 3 sc, skip 8 sts, 6 sc, skip 8 sts, 3 sc. (12 sts)
Break the working yarn in Blue, leaving a long tail, and thread through to the outside. It will later be used to close the remaining opening.
Rnds 22–35: 1 sc in every st of the prev rnd. (12 sts)
Stuff the part worked in Linen (Rnds 21–35) with fiberfill.

Rnd 36: [Dec 1] 6 times. (6 sts)
Break the working yarn and use a tapestry needle to thread it through the remaining 6 sts and cinch closed. Secure the yarn and weave it in.

Finishing

» With the Blue tail and a tapestry needle, use the overcast stitch to sew the openings along Rnd 20 together, stitch for stitch.

AT THE Doctor's Office

When you are sick, you need to be thoroughly checked. Our doctors will measure your blood pressure, listen to your lungs, and take your temperature. Wounds are dressed with bandages and Band-Aids, and if nothing else helps, you will be given a shot.

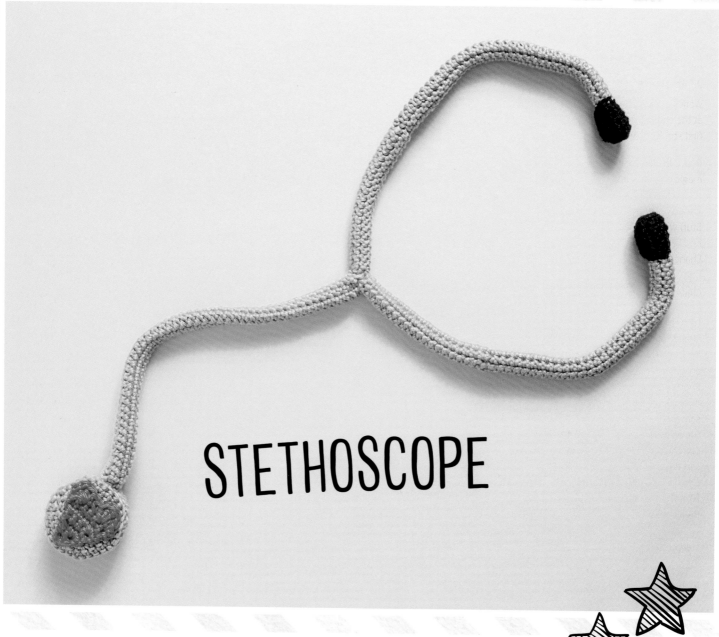

STETHOSCOPE

Materials

» #2 fine weight cotton yarn; shown in Woll Butt Camilla, 100% cotton, 138 yd/125 m per 1.75 oz/50 g skein, in colors/amounts as follows:
  » Grey, approx 27.6 yd/25 m, 0.35 oz/10 g
  » Dusty Pink, approx 27.6 yd/25 m, 0.35 oz/10 g
  » Black, approx 15.8 yd/12.5 m, 0.2 oz/5 g
  » Red, remnant

» Crochet hook, 2.5 mm
» Polyester fiberfill
» Pipe cleaners or craft wire
» Adhesive tape
» Tapestry needle

Earpiece, Ear Tube and Upper Tubing Combination (make 2)

Work in rnds. At the beginning of every rnd, ch1; at the end of every rnd, join with a sl-st into the first stitch of the rnd. Do not turn work.

Rnd 1: In Black, work 6 sc into an adjustable magic ring. (6 sts)
Rnd 2: [1 sc, inc 1] 3 times. (9 sts)
Rnds 3–5: 1 sc in every st of the prev rnd. (9 sts) Stuff with fiberfill.
Rnd 6: [1 sc, dec 1] 3 times. (6 sts)
Change to Grey.
Rnd 7: Working into the back loop of the stitch only, 1 sc in every st of the prev rnd. (6 sts)
Rnds 8–40: 1 sc in every st of the prev rnd. (6 sts)
Change to Dusty Pink.
Rnd 41: Working into the front loop of the stitch only, 1 sc in every st of the prev rnd. (6 sts) Shorten the pipe cleaner or craft wire to approx 4.7 in/12 cm (the piece of wire should have the same length as the grey crocheted part). Bend the ends, and wrap them with adhesive tape for protection to prevent any sharp points. Now, insert the wire into the crocheted piece.
Rnds 42–60: 1 sc in every st of the prev rnd. (6 sts)
Break the working yarn, leaving a long tail.

Lower Tubing

Work in rnds. At the beginning of every rnd, ch1; at the end of every rnd, join with a sl-st into the first stitch of the rnd. Do not turn work.

Rnd 1: In Dusty Pink, crochet a chain of 6, and join the chain into the round with a sl-st into the first chain (6 sts). Leave a long beginning tail.
Rnd 2: 1 sc in every ch. (6 sts)
Rnds 3–50: 1 sc in every st of the prev rnd. (6 sts)
Break the working yarn, leaving a longer end.

Chest Piece

Work in rnds. At the beginning of every rnd, ch1; at the end of every rnd, join with a sl-st into the first stitch of the rnd. Do not turn work.

Rnd 1: In Grey, work 6 sc into an adjustable magic ring. (6 sts)
Rnd 2: [Inc 1] 6 times. (12 sts)
Rnd 3: [1 sc, inc 1] 6 times. (18 sts)
Rnd 4: [2 sc, inc 1] 6 times. (24 sts)
Rnd 5: [3 sc, inc 1] 6 times. (30 sts)
Rnd 6: Working into the back loop of the stitch only, 1 sc in every st of the prev rnd. (30 sts)
Rnds 7–8: 1 sc in every st of the prev rnd. (30 sts)
Rnd 9: Working into the back loop of the stitch only, [3 sc, dec 1] 6 times. (24 sts)
Rnd 10: [2 sc, dec 1] 6 times. (18 sts)
Rnd 11: [1 sc, dec 1] 6 times. (12 sts)
Stuff with fiberfill.
Rnd 12: [Dec 1] 6 times. (6 sts)
Break the working yarn and, using a tapestry needle, thread through all 6 sts. Cinch to close the opening. Secure the yarn to finish off, and hide the end on the inside of the crocheted piece.

Heart Appliqué

Work in back-and-forth rows with turning. At the end of every row, ch1, and then turn work.

In Red, crochet a chain of 2.
Row 1: Work 2 sc in the 2nd ch from the hook. (2 sts)
Row 2: 1 sc in every st of the prev row. (2 sts)
Row 3: [Inc 1] 2 times. (4 sts)
Row 4: 1 sc in every st of the prev row. (4 sts)
Row 5: Inc 1, 2 sc, inc 1. (6 sts)
Row 6: 1 sc in every st of the prev row. (6 sts)
Row 7: 1 sc into the first stitch of the prev row, (1 hdc, 2 dc, 1 hdc) in the 2nd st of the prev row, dec 1 (sc the 3rd and 4th sts together), (1 hdc, 2 dc, 1 hdc) in the 5th st of the prev row, 1 sc in the last st of the prev row. (11 sts)
Break the working yarn, leaving a long tail.

Finishing

» Sew the Dusty Pink ends of the 2 earpieces and the ear tube and upper tubing combination pieces (upper tubing part) together at the openings (Rnd 60) stitch by stitch. Now, sew the lower tubing (Rnd 50) onto this seam in overcast stitch. Using the long beginning tail, sew the chest piece to the end of the lower tubing in overcast stitch at the level of Rnds 6–8. At the end, working in basting stitch, sew the heart appliqué onto the front of the chest piece. Secure all ends and weave in the tails on the inside of the stethoscope. Bend the upper tubing parts into the required shape.

AT THE DOCTOR'S OFFICE

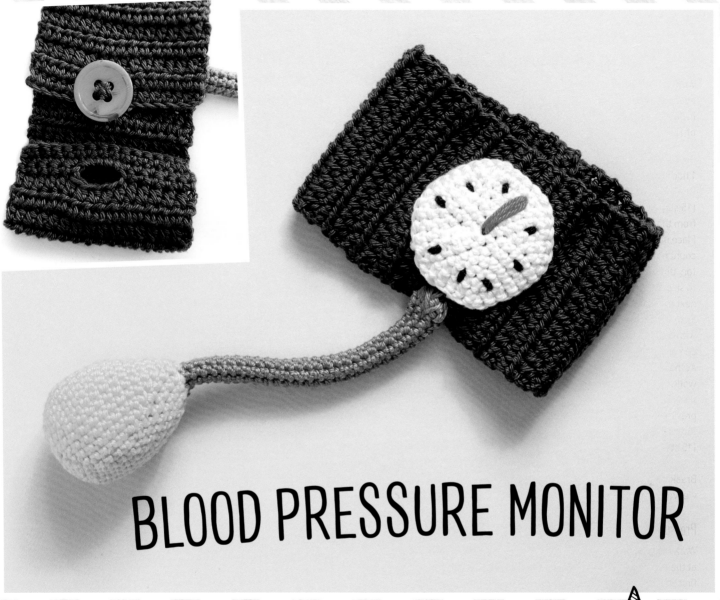

BLOOD PRESSURE MONITOR

Materials

» #2 fine weight cotton yarn; shown in Schachenmayr Catania, 100% cotton, 138 yd/125 m per 1.75 oz/50 g skein, in colors/amounts as follows:
  » Jeans, approx 27.6 yd/25 m, 0.35 oz/10 g
  » Sun, approx 15.8 yd/12.5 m, 0.2 oz/5 g
» #2 fine weight cotton yarn; shown in Woll Butt Camilla, 100% cotton, 138 yd/125 m per 1.75 oz/50 g skein, in colors/amounts as follows:
  » Blue, approx 15.8 yd/12.5 m, 0.2 oz/5 g

» White, approx 15.8 yd/12.5 m, 0.2 oz/5 g
» Remnants in Black and Red
» Crochet hooks, 2.5 mm and 3.0 mm
» Polyester fiberfill
» Tapestry needle
» Button

Cuff

Work in back-and-forth rows with turning. End every row with ch2; then turn work.
In Jeans and with 3.0 mm hook, crochet a chain of 17.

Row 1: Work 1 hdc in the 3rd ch from the hook, 1 hdc in every following ch. (15 sts)
Rows 2–35: 1 hdc in every st of the prev row (15 sts). End the last row with only ch1, since from the next row on, work continues in sc. Place your button onto the crocheted piece and count how many sts equal the width of the button. Determine this way how many sts you need to skip for the buttonhole in the middle of the next row, and adjust the stitch count accordingly. In the pictured sample, I have used a button with a diameter of 0.8 in/2 cm, so I've worked ch4 and skipped 4 sts of the prev row.
At the end of all following rows, ch1 and turn work.
Row 36: 5 sc, ch4, skip the next 4 sts of the prev row, 6 sc. (15 sts)
Row 37: 6 sc, 4 sc in ch-sp of the prev row, 5 sc. (15 sts)
Row 38: 1 sc in every st of the prev row. (15 sts)
Break the working yarn, secure, and carefully weave in the end.

Pressure Gauge

Work in rnds. At the beginning of every rnd, ch1; at the end of every rnd, join with a sl-st into the first stitch of the rnd. Do not turn work.

Rnd 1: In White and with 3.0 mm hook, work 6 sc into an adjustable magic ring. (6 sts)
Rnd 2: [Inc 1] 6 times. (12 sts)
Rnd 3: [1 sc, inc 1] 6 times. (18 sts)
Rnd 4: [2 sc, inc 1] 6 times. (24 sts)
Rnd 5: [3 sc, inc 1] 6 times. (30 sts)
Rnd 6: [4 sc, inc 1] 6 times. (36 sts)
Break the working yarn, leaving a long tail.

Inflation Bulb

Work in rnds. At the beginning of every rnd, ch1; at the end of every rnd, join with a sl-st into the first stitch of the rnd. Do not turn work.

Rnd 1: In Sun and with 2.5 mm hook, 6 sc into an adjustable magic ring. (6 sts)
Rnd 2: [Inc 1] 6 times. (12 sts)
Rnd 3: [1 sc, inc 1] 6 times. (18 sts)
Rnd 4: [2 sc, inc 1] 6 times. (24 sts)
Rnd 5: [3 sc, inc 1] 6 times. (30 sts)
Rnds 6–10: 1 sc in every st of the prev rnd. (30 sts)
Rnd 11: [8 sc, dec 1] 3 times. (27 sts)
Rnd 12: [7 sc, dec 1] 3 times. (24 sts)
Rnd 13: [6 sc, dec 1] 3 times. (21 sts)
Rnd 14: [5 sc, dec 1] 3 times. (18 sts)
Rnd 15: [4 sc, dec 1] 3 times. (15 sts)
Rnd 16: [3 sc, dec 1] 3 times. (12 sts)
Stuff with fiberfill.
Rnd 17: [Dec 1] 6 times. (6 sts)
Change to Blue.
Rnds 18–35: 1 sc in every st of the prev rnd. (6 sts)
Break the working yarn, leaving a long tail.

Finishing

» Use Jeans to sew the button to the middle of the cuff at the level of Rows 1–2. In Red, embroider a hand onto the pressure gauge in backstitch over Rnds 1–5, and in Black, embroider 8 small gradation marks evenly distributed throughout Rnd 5. Now, using the white tail and working in basting stitch, sew the pressure gauge to the middle of the cuff over Rows 18–24. Using the long tail, sew the inflation bulb to the cuff next to the pressure gauge at the level of Rows 20–21. Finish off by securing all ends; then hide the tails.

Tip

The finished size of the blood pressure monitor can be easily adjusted by either working additional rnds of 15 hdc after Row 35 or by ending work earlier.

SYRINGE

Materials

» #2 fine weight cotton yarn; shown in Woll Butt Camilla, 100% cotton, 138 yd/125 m per 1.75 oz/50 g skein, in colors/amounts as follows:
  » White, approx 15.8 yd/12.5 m, 0.2 oz/5 g
  » Remnants in Grey, Blue, and Black
» Crochet hook, 2.5 mm
» Polyester fiberfill
» Tapestry needle

Instructions

Work in rnds. At the beginning of every rnd, ch1; at the end of every rnd, join with a sl-st into the first stitch of the rnd. Do not turn work.

Rnd 1: In Grey, work 4 sc into an adjustable magic ring. (4 sts)
Rnds 2–4: 1 sc in every st of the prev rnd. (4 sts) Change to White.
Rnd 5: [1 sc, inc 1] 2 times. (6 sts)
Rnd 6: [1 sc, inc 1] 3 times. (9 sts)
Rnd 7: [2 sc, inc 1] 3 times. (12 sts)
Rnds 8–20: 1 sc in every st of the prev rnd. (12 sts)
Rnd 21a: Working into the front loop of the stitch only, [1 sc, inc 1] 6 times. (18 sts)
Rnd 22a: Working into the sts of Rnd 21a, 2 sc, inc 1, 3 sl-st, 2 sc, [inc 1] 2 times, 2 sc, 3 sl-st, 2 sc, inc 1. (22 sts)

Break the working yarn in White, secure, and weave in the end.
Stuff the syringe with fiberfill.
Attach new working yarn in Blue to Rnd 20, and work as follows into the inner, unused loops of the sts only:
Rnd 21b: Working into the back loop of the stitch only, 1 sc in every st of the prev rnd. (12 sts)
Rnd 22b: Working into the sts of Rnd 21b, 1 sc in every st of the prev rnd. (12 sts)
Rnd 23: 1 sc in every st of the prev rnd. (12 sts)
Rnd 24: Working into the front loop of the stitch only, [1 sc, inc 1] 6 times. (18 sts)
Rnd 25: Working into the back loop of the stitch only, 1 sc in every st of the prev rnd. (18 sts)
Rnd 26: Working into the back loop of the stitch only, [1 sc, dec 1] 6 times. (12 sts)

Stuff the remaining space of the syringe with fiberfill, too.
Rnd 27: [Dec 1] 6 times. (6 sts)
Break the working yarn, thread it through all 6 sts, and cinch the opening closed. Now, secure the end, and weave it in on the inside.

Finishing

» In Black, embroider gradation marks onto the syringe at the level of Rnds 9–18 with a tapestry needle in basting stitch as follows: Embroider over 4 sts once and then over 2 sts twice; repeat 2 more times, and end going over 4 sts, as shown in the photo. Secure the end, and weave in the tail.

THERMOMETER

Materials

- » #2 fine weight cotton yarn; shown in Woll Butt Camilla, 100% cotton, 138 yd/125 m per 1.75 oz/50 g skein, in colors/amounts as follows:
  - » Emerald, approx 15.8 yd/12.5 m, 0.2 oz/5 g
  - » Grey, approx 15.8 yd/12.5 m, 0.2 oz/5 g
  - » Remnants in Black, Red, and Green
- » Crochet hook, 2.5 mm
- » Polyester fiberfill
- » Tapestry needle

Instructions

Thermometer

Work in rnds. At the beginning of every rnd, ch1; at the end of every rnd, join with a sl-st into the first stitch of the rnd. Do not turn work.

Rnd 1: In Grey, work 6 sc into an adjustable magic ring. (6 sts)
Rnds 2–5: 1 sc in every st of the prev rnd. (6 sts) Change to Emerald.
Rnd 6: 1 sc in every st of the prev rnd. (6 sts)
Rnd 7: 1 sc, inc 1, 2 sc, inc 1, 1 sc. (8 sts)
Rnd 8: 2 sc, inc 1, 3 sc, inc 1, 1 sc. (10 sts)
Rnd 9: 2 sc, inc 1, 4 sc, inc 1, 2 sc. (12 sts)
Rnd 10: 2 sc, inc 1, 5 sc, inc 1, 3 sc. (14 sts)
Rnd 11: 3 sc, inc 1, 6 sc, inc 1, 3 sc. (16 sts)
Rnds 12–26: 1 sc in every st of the prev rnd. (16 sts)

Rnd 27: 3 sc, dec 1, 6 sc, dec 1, 3 sc. (14 sts)
Stuff the thermometer lightly with fiberfill, and pat it flat.
Break the working yarn, leaving a long tail, and, inserting the needle through the outer loops of the sts only, sew the sts of the opening closed 1 to 1 in overcast stitch.

Display Window

Work in back-and-forth rows with turning. End every row with ch1; then turn work.
In Grey, crochet a chain of 9.
Row 1: Work 1 sc in the 2nd ch from the hook, 1 sc in every following st. (8 sts)
Rows 2–3: 1 sc in every st of the prev row. (8 sts)
Break the working yarn, leaving a long tail.

Finishing

- » In Black, embroider the desired number onto the display in backstitch, and then make a French knot for the degree sign. In Red and Green, embroider 2 little indicator lights over the width of 1 st each to the left of the number in basting stitch. Sew the display window onto the thermometer in basting stitch at the level of Rnds 16–23. Secure the yarn, and weave in all ends.

OTOSCOPE

Materials

- » #2 fine weight cotton yarn; shown in Schachenmayr Catania, 100% cotton, 138 yd/ 125 m per 1.75 oz/50 g skein, in colors/amounts as follows:
  - » Sun, approx 27.6 yd/25 m, 0.35 oz/10 g
- » Crochet hook, 2.5 mm
- » Polyester fiberfill
- » Tapestry needle

Instructions

Work in rnds. At the beginning of every rnd, ch1; at the end of every rnd, join with a sl-st into the first stitch of the rnd. Do not turn work.

Ear Probe

Rnd 1: In Sun, ch6, and join the chain into the round with a sl-st into the first chain. (6 sts)
Rnd 2: Work 9 sc around the chain ring. (9 sts)
Rnds 3–4: 1 sc in every st of the prev rnd. (9 sts)
Rnd 5: [2 sc, inc 1] 3 times. (12 sts)
Rnds 6–7: 1 sc in every st of the prev rnd. (12 sts)
Rnd 8: [3 sc, inc 1] 3 times. (15 sts)
Rnds 9–10: 1 sc in every st of the prev rnd. (15 sts)
Rnd 11: [4 sc, inc 1] 3 times. (18 sts)
Rnds 12–13: 1 sc in every st of the prev rnd. (18 sts)
Break the working yarn, secure, and weave in the end.

Handle

Rnd 1: In Sun, work 6 sc into an adjustable magic ring. (6 sts)
Rnd 2: [Inc 1] 6 times. (12 sts)
Rnds 3–17: 1 sc in every st of the prev rnd. (12 sts)
Now, stuff the handle with fiberfill.
Rnd 18: [2 sc, dec 1] 3 times. (9 sts)
From here on, continue in rows. End every row with ch1; then turn.
Row 19: Ch1, turn, 1 sc in each of the next 4 sts. (4 sts)
Rows 20–35: 1 sc in every st of the prev row. (4 sts)
Break the yarn, leaving a long tail.

Tip

The handle may be crocheted in spiral rounds instead.

Finishing

- » Wrap Rows 20–35 of the handles around Rnds 6–9 of the ear probes, and sew the 2 pieces together in basting stitch. Sew Row 35 of the handles to the 5 unused sts from Rnd 18 of the ear probes in mattress stitch. If needed, close the side openings in mattress stitch. Secure the end, and hide the tail on the inside.

REFLEX HAMMER

Materials

» #2 fine weight cotton yarn; shown in Woll Butt Camilla, 100% cotton, 138 yd/125 m per 1.75 oz/50 g skein, in colors/amounts as follows:
  » Grey, approx 15.8 yd/12.5 m, 0.2 oz/5 g
  » Light Green, approx 15.8 yd/12.5 m, 0.2 oz/5 g
» Crochet hook, 2.5 mm
» Polyester fiberfill
» Tapestry needle

Instructions

Work in rnds. At the beginning of every rnd, ch1; at the end of every rnd, join with a sl-st into the first stitch of the rnd. Do not turn work.

Rubber Head

Rnd 1: In Grey, work 6 sc into an adjustable magic ring. (6 sts)
Rnd 2: [1 sc, inc 1] 3 times. (9 sts)
Rnd 3: 1 sc in every st of the prev rnd. (9 sts)
Rnd 4: [2 sc, inc 1] 3 times. (12 sts)
Rnd 5: 1 sc in every st of the prev rnd. (12 sts)
Rnd 6: [3 sc, inc 1] 3 times. (15 sts)
Rnd 7: 1 sc in every st of the prev rnd. (15 sts)
Rnd 8: [4 sc, inc 1] 3 times. (18 sts)
Rnd 9: 1 sc in every st of the prev rnd. (18 sts)
Rnd 10: [5 sc, inc 1] 3 times. (21 sts)
Rnds 11–15: 1 sc in every st of the prev rnd. (21 sts)

Break the working yarn, leaving a long tail; then stuff the rubber head only lightly with fiberfill, and shape it. Now, close the opening with a tapestry needle in overcast stitch, inserting the needle through the outer loops of the sts only.

Tip

The rubber head can be worked in spiral rounds instead.

Handle

Rnd 1: In Light Green, work 6 sc into an adjustable magic ring. (6 sts)
Rnd 2: [Inc 1] 6 times. (12 sts)
Rnds 3–17: 1 sc in every st of the prev rnd. (12 sts)
Now, stuff the handle with fiberfill.
Rnd 18: [2 sc, dec 1] 3 times. (9 sts)

From here on, continue in rows. End every row with ch1, and turn work.
Row 19: Ch1, turn, 1 sc ea in next 4 sts. (4 sts)
Rows 20–38: 1 sc in every st of the prev row. (4 sts)
Break the yarn, leaving a long tail.

Finishing

» Wrap Rows 20–38 of the handle around Rnds 8–11 of the rubber head, and sew the 2 pieces together in basting stitch. Additionally, sew Rnd 38 of the handle to the 5 unused sts of Rnd 18 of the rubber head in mattress stitch. If needed, close the side openings in mattress stitch. Secure the end, and hide the tail on the inside.

TONGUE DEPRESSOR

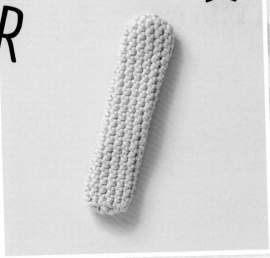

Materials

» #2 fine weight cotton yarn; shown in Woll Butt Camilla, 100% cotton, 138 yd/125 m
   per 1.75 oz/50 g skein, in colors/amounts as follows:
   » Linen, approx 15.8 yd/12.5 m, 0.2 oz/5 g
» Crochet hook, 2.5 mm
» Tapestry needle

Instructions

Work in rnds. At the beginning of every rnd, ch1; at the end of every rnd, join with a sl-st into the first stitch of the rnd. Do not turn work.

Rnd 1: In Linen, work 6 sc into an adjustable magic ring. (6 sts)
Rnd 2: [Inc 1] 6 times. (12 sts)
Rnds 3–24: 1 sc in every st of the prev rnd. (12 sts)
Rnd 25: [Dec 1] 6 times. (6 sts)

Finishing

» Break the working yarn, and thread it through all 6 sts with a tapestry needle. Cinch to close the opening. Secure the end of the yarn, and hide the tail on the inside of the crocheted piece. Pat the tongue depressor flat to shape it.

Tip

If desired, the tongue depressor can be worked in spiral rounds instead.

BANDAGE & BAND-AID

Materials

Bandage

» #2 fine weight cotton yarn; shown in Woll Butt Camilla, 100% cotton, 138 yd/125 m per 1.75 oz/50 g skein, in colors/amounts as follows:
  » White, approx 39.4 yd/37.5 m, 0.5 oz/15 g

Band-Aid

» #2 fine weight cotton yarn; shown in Woll Butt Camilla, 100% cotton, 138 yd/125 m per 1.75 oz/50 g skein, in colors/amounts as follows:
  » Caramel, approx 15.8 yd/12.5 m, 0.2 oz/5 g
  » White, approx 15.8 yd/12.5 m, 0.2 oz/5 g

For Both

» Crochet hooks, 2.5 mm and 3.0 mm
» Tapestry needle

Instructions

BANDAGE

Work in back-and-forth rows with turning. End every row with ch2; then turn work.

In White, and working with 3.0 mm hook, crochet a chain of 14.
Row 1: Work 1 hdc in the 3rd ch from the hook, 1 hdc in every following ch. (12 sts)
Rows 2–40: 1 hdc in every st of the prev row. (12 sts)

Finishing

» Secure the end, and weave it in under the sts.

Tip

The length of the bandage can be adjusted as needed by crocheting more rows as described above. However, please be sure to make the bandage short enough not to pose a strangulation hazard to the child.

BAND-AID

Work in back-and-forth rows with turning. End every row with ch1; then turn work.

In Caramel, and working with 2.5 mm hook, crochet a chain of 9.
Row 1: Work 1 sc in the 2nd ch from the hook, 1 sc in every following ch. (8 sts)
Rows 2–6: 1 sc in every st of the prev row. (8 sts)
Row 7a: Working into the back loop of the stitch only, 1 sc in every st of the prev row. (8 sts)
Rows 8–11a: Working into the back loop of the stitch only, 1 sc in every st of the prev row. (8 sts)
Pull the last loop long to secure, and put the working yarn in Caramel aside, but don't cut it yet.
Attach new working yarn in White to the unused loop of the st after Row 6.

Row 7b: Working into the front loop of the stitch only, 1 sc in every st of the prev row. (8 sts)
Rows 8–11b: Working into the front loop of the stitch only, 1 sc in every st of the prev row. (8 sts)
Break the working yarn in White, leaving a long tail, and secure the last st. Now, take up the working yarn in Caramel again.
Row 12: Crochet both pieces together, working 8 sc. (8 sts)
Rows 13–17: 1 sc in every st of the prev row. (8 sts)
Break the working yarn, secure the end, and weave it in under the sts.

Finishing

» Using the white tail, embroider 4 dots on the top side of the Band-Aid with French knots. Finish off the working yarn in White, and weave in the end.

PRESCRIPTION BOTTLE

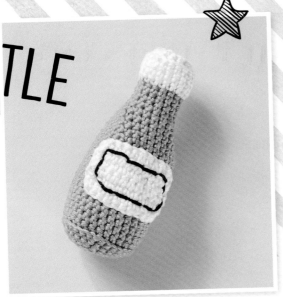

Materials

» #2 fine weight cotton yarn; shown in Woll Butt Camilla, 100% cotton, 138 yd/125 m per 1.75 oz/50 g skein, in colors/amounts as follows:
  » Caramel, approx 39.4 yd/37.5 m, 0.5 oz/15 g
  » White, approx 15.8 yd/12.5 m, 0.2 oz/5 g
  » Black, remnant
» Crochet hook, 2.5 mm
» Polyester fiberfill
» Tapestry needle

Instructions

Bottle

Work in rnds. At the beginning of every rnd, ch1; at the end of every rnd, join with a sl-st into the first stitch of the rnd. Do not turn work.

Rnd 1: In Caramel, work 6 sc into an adjustable magic ring. (6 sts)
Rnd 2: [Inc 1] 6 times. (12 sts)
Rnd 3: [1 sc, inc 1] 6 times. (18 sts)
Rnd 4: [2 sc, inc 1] 6 times. (24 sts)
Rnd 5: [3 sc, inc 1] 6 times. (30 sts)
Rnd 6: Working into the back loop of the stitch only, 1 sc in every st of the prev rnd. (30 sts)
Rnds 7–17: 1 sc in every st of the prev rnd. (30 sts)
Rnd 18: [8 sc, dec 1] 3 times. (27 sts)
Rnd 19: [7 sc, dec 1] 3 times. (24 sts)
Rnd 20: [6 sc, dec 1] 3 times. (21 sts)
Rnd 21: [5 sc, dec 1] 3 times. (18 sts)
Rnd 22: [4 sc, dec 1] 3 times. (15 sts)
Rnds 23–25: 1 sc in every st of the prev rnd. (15 sts)

Change to White.
Rnd 26: Working into the front loop of the stitch only, [4 sc, inc 1] 3 times. (18 sts)
Rnds 27–28: 1 sc in every st of the prev rnd. (18 sts)
Stuff the bottle with fiberfill.
Rnd 29: Working into the back loop of the stitch only, [1 sc, dec 1] 6 times. (12 sts)
Rnd 30: [Dec 1] 6 times. (6 sts)
Break the working yarn and, using a tapestry needle, thread through all 6 sts. Cinch to close the opening. Secure the yarn to finish off, and hide the end on the inside.

Label

Work in back-and-forth rows with turning. End every row with ch1; then turn work.

In White, crochet a chain of 11.

Row 1: Work 1 sc in the 2nd ch from the hook, 1 sc in every following ch. (10 sts)

Rows 2–4: 1 sc in every st of the prev row (10 sts). After having completed the last row, don't turn work.
Crochet an edging around the whole piece, working 1 rnd of sc, starting with ch1, 3 sc along each of the 2 short sides, 8 sc at each of the long sides, and 2 sc into each of the 4 corner sts; join into the rnd with a sl-st into the first stitch. (30 sts)
Break the working yarn, leaving a long tail, and secure the end.

Finishing

» In Black, embroider a decorative frame onto the label in backstitch, approx 0.2 in/0.5 cm in from the edge. Using the white tail, sew the label to the bottle at the level of Rnds 10–17 in basting stitch.

PILL BLISTER PACK

Materials

» #2 fine weight cotton yarn; shown in Woll Butt Camilla, 100% cotton, 138 yd/125 m per 1.75 oz/50 g skein, in colors/amounts as follows:
  » White, approx 27.6 yd/25 m, 0.35 oz/10 g
  » Yellow, approx 15.8 yd/12.5 m, 0.2 oz/5 g
  » Orange, approx 15.8 yd/12.5 m, 0.2 oz/5 g
  » Grey, remnant
» Crochet hook, 2.5 mm
» Tapestry needle

Instructions

Blister Pack

Work in back-and-forth rows with turning. End every row with ch1; then turn work.

In White, crochet a chain of 16.
Row 1: Work 1 sc in the 2nd ch from the hook, 1 sc in every following ch. (15 sts)
Rows 2–19: 1 sc in every st of the prev row (15 sts). After having completed the last row, don't turn work.
Crochet an edging around the whole piece, working 1 rnd of sc, starting with ch1, work 18 sc along each of the 2 sides, 13 sc at each of the top and bottom edge, and 2 sc into each of the 4 corner sts; join into the rnd with a sl-st into the first stitch. (70 sts)
Break the working yarn, secure the end, and weave it in under the sts.

Yellow Pills (make 4)

Work in rnds. At the beginning of every rnd, ch1; at the end of every rnd, join with a sl-st into the first stitch of the rnd. Do not turn work.
Rnd 1: In Yellow, work 5 sc into an adjustable magic ring. (5 sts)
Rnd 2: [Inc 1] 5 times. (10 sts)
Rnd 3: 1 sc in every st of the prev rnd. (10 sts)
Break the yarn, leaving a long tail.

Orange Pills (make 4)

Work in rnds. At the beginning of every rnd, ch1; at the end of every rnd, join with a sl-st into the first stitch of the rnd. Do not turn work.

In Orange, crochet a chain of 6.
Rnd 1: Work 1 sc in the 2nd ch from the hook, 1 sc in each of next 3 chains, 2 sc in the last ch, and then continue into the unused loops on the other side of the chain: 1 sc in every ch. (10 sts)
Rnd 2: 1 sc in every st of the prev rnd. (10 sts)
Break the yarn, leaving a long tail.

Finishing

» Sew 8 pills evenly distributed onto the blister pack in overcast stitch. Now, embroider decorative lines between individual pills in Grey with a tapestry needle. Secure the yarn, and weave in all ends.

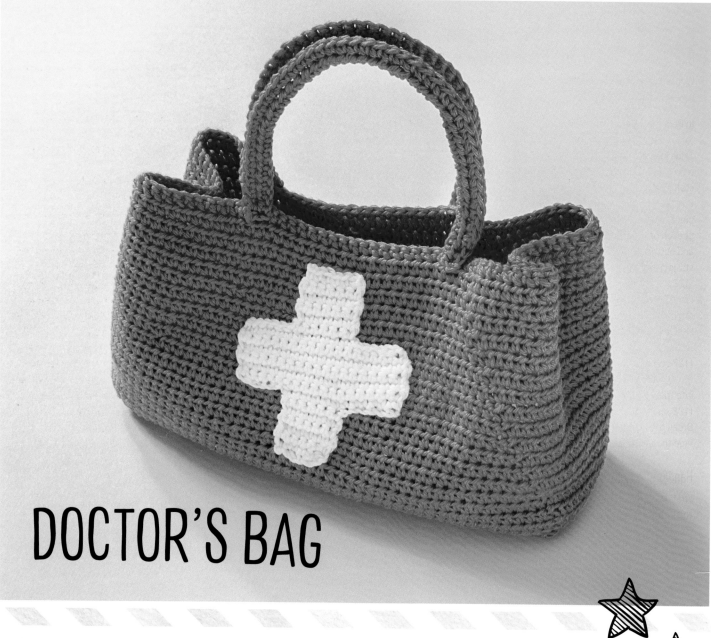

DOCTOR'S BAG

Materials

- » #2 fine weight cotton yarn; shown in Woll Butt Camilla, 100% cotton, 138 yd/125 m per 1.75 oz/50 g skein, in colors/amounts as follows:
  - » Red, approx 213 yd/187.5 m, 2.7 oz/75 g
  - » White, approx 15.8 yd/12.5 m, 0.2 oz/5 g
- » Crochet hook, 3.0 mm
- » Tapestry needle

Bag

Work hdc in back-and forth-rows. End every row with ch2; then turn.

In Red, crochet a chain of 47.
Row 1: Work 1 hdc in the 3rd ch from the hook, 1 hdc in every following ch. (45 sts)
Rows 2–9: 1 hdc in every st of the prev row (45 sts). At the end of the last row, do not turn!
Rnd 10: Ch1. Crochet an edging around the piece, working a total of 122 sc, of these, 14 sc at each of the 2 sides, 43 sc at each of the top and bottom, and 2 sc into each of the 4 corner sts; join into the rnd with a sl-st into the first st. (122 sts)
From here on, continue in rnds in hdc. Begin every rnd with ch2, and end every round with 1 sl-st into the first stitch. Do not turn work.
Rnds 11–29: 1 hdc in every st of the prev rnd. (122 sts)
Rnd 30: Ch1, 1 sc in every st of the prev rnd; join into the rnd with a sl-st into the first stitch. (122 sts)
Break the working yarn, secure the end, and hide the tail on the inside.

Handles (make 2)

Work in back-and-forth rows with turning. At the end of Row 1, ch1, and turn work.

In Red, crochet a chain of 47.
Row 1: Work 1 hdc in the 3rd ch from the hook, 1 hdc in every following ch. (45 sts)
Row 2: 1 sc in every st of the prev row. (45 sts)
Break the yarn, leaving a long tail.

Cross (make 2)

Work in back-and-forth rows with turning. If not otherwise stated, end the row with ch1; then turn work.

In White, crochet a chain of 7.
Row 1: Work 1 sc in the 2nd ch from the hook, 1 sc in every following ch. (6 sts)
Rows 2–5: 1 sc in every st of the prev row. (6 sts)
Row 6: 1 sc in every st of the prev row, ch7 (13 sts). Turn without a turning chain.
Row 7: 1 sc in the 2nd ch from the hook, 1 sc in every following ch, 1 sc in every sc of the prev row, ch7 (19 sts). Turn without a turning chain.
Row 8: 1 sc in the 2nd ch from the hook, 1 sc in every following ch, 1 sc in every sc of the prev row. (18 sts)
Rows 9–12: 1 sc in every st of the prev row (18 sts). Turn without a turning chain.
Row 13: 1 sl-st into the first 6 sts of the prev row, 1 sc in every following st of the prev row (18 sts). Turn without a turning chain.

Row 14: 1 sl-st into the first 6 sts of the prev row, 1 sc in every sc of the prev row, leaving the sl-sts of the prev row unworked. (12 sts)
Row 15: 1 sc in every sc of the prev row, here, too, leaving the sl-sts of the prev row unworked. (6 sts)
Rows 16–19: 1 sc in every st of the prev row. (6 sts)
Break the yarn, leaving a long tail.

Finishing

» Using a tapestry needle, sew the 2 handles to the bag in mattress stitch evenly over a width of 3 sts each in the middle of the side panels as follows: For ease of work, mark the spots with a stitch marker or piece of contrasting yarn before you start attaching the handles. The 2 ends of the same handle should be spaced 15 sts from each other, and each of the 2 handles 40 sts from the other handle. Now, sew the 2 crosses to the bag below the handles in basting stitch, approx at the level of Rnds 15–28 of the bag. Secure the yarn, and weave in all ends.

AT THE
Police
Station

Watch out . . . traffic stop ahead! With our hand signal, we'll flag down every third car. Documents are thoroughly checked. When a lawbreaker is spotted, we'll put him in handcuffs. If needed, we can use a walkie-talkie to call for backup.

HANDCUFFS

Materials

- » #2 fine weight cotton yarn; shown in Woll Butt Camilla, 100% cotton, 138 yd/125 m per 1.75 oz/50 g skein, in colors/amounts as follows:
  - » Grey, approx 55.2 yd/50 m, 0.7 oz/20 g
  - » Black, remnant
- » Crochet hook, 2.5 mm
- » Tapestry needle

Instructions

Handcuffs (make 2)

Work in rnds. At the beginning of every rnd, ch1; at the end of every rnd, join with a sl-st into the first stitch of the rnd. Do not turn work.

Rnd 1: In Grey, work 9 sc into an adjustable magic ring. (9 sts)
Rnds 2–50: 1 sc in every st of the prev rnd. (9 sts)
Break the working yarn, leaving a long end, and sew Rnds 1 and 50 together in overcast stitch, forming a ring.

Tip

The size of the handcuffs can be adapted by working more or fewer rounds.

Lock (make 2)

Work in rnds. At the beginning of every rnd, ch1; at the end of every rnd, join with a sl-st into the first stitch of the rnd. Do not turn work.

In Grey, crochet a chain of 8.
Rnd 1: Work 1 sc in the 2nd ch from the hook, 1 sc in each of next 5 chains, 3 sc in the last ch, and then continue into the unused loops on the other side of the chain, 1 sc in each of next 5 chains, 2 sc in the last ch of this side. Join the rnd with 1 sl-st into the first stitch. (16 sts)
Rnds 2–5: 1 sc in every st of the prev rnd. (16 sts)
Break the working yarn, leaving a long tail.

Chain

Work in rnds. At the beginning of every rnd, ch1; at the end of every rnd, join with a sl-st into the first stitch of the rnd. Do not turn work.
On this piece, leave a long beginning tail.

Rnd 1: In Grey, work 6 sc into an adjustable magic ring. (6 sts)
Rnds 2–25: 1 sc in every st of the prev rnd. (6 sts)
Break the working yarn, leaving a long tail.

Keyhole (make 4)

Rnd 1: In Black, work 5 sc into an adjustable magic ring. (5 sts)
From here on, continue in rows. End every row with ch1; then turn work.
Row 2: Work ch1, and turn work, crochet 1 sc in the next st of the prev row. (1 st)
Row 3: 1 sc in the st of the prev row. (1 st)
Break the working yarn, leaving a long tail.

Finishing

- » Sew 2 locks each in overcast stitch on the outside of one handcuff. Using the beginning and ending tails, sew the ends of the chain to the locks in overcast stitch at the level of Rnd 1. Sew 2 keyholes to each lock at the level of Rnds 1–5 in basting stitch, 1 on each side of the lock. Finish off and secure the end; then hide all tails.

TRAFFIC PADDLE

Materials

- » #2 fine weight cotton yarn; shown in Woll Butt Camilla, 100% cotton, 138 yd/ 125 m per 1.75 oz/50 g skein, in colors/amounts as follows:
    - » White, approx 71 yd/62.5 m, 0.9 oz/25 g
    - » Green, approx 27.6 yd/25 m, 0.35 oz/10 g
    - » Red, approx 27.6 yd/25 m, 0.35 oz/10 g
- » Crochet hook, 2.5 mm
- » Polyester fiberfill
- » Tapestry needle

Instructions

Handle

Work starts in the round. At the beginning of every rnd, ch1; at the end of every rnd, join with a sl-st into the first stitch of the rnd. Do not turn work.

Rnd 1: In White, work 6 sc into an adjustable magic ring. (6 sts)

Rnd 2: [Inc 1] 6 times. (12 sts)

Rnds 3–30: 1 sc in every st of the prev rnd. (12 sts)

Stuff the handle gradually with fiberfill, and nudge it into a rounded shape.

From here on, continue in rows. End every row with ch1; then turn.

Row 31: Ch1, turn work, and work 1 sc in each of next 6 sts. (6 sts)

Row 32: 1 sc in every st of the prev row. (6 sts)

Break the working yarn, leaving a longer end. Attach new working yarn to Rnd 30 and, working over the unused 6 sts, repeat Rows 31–32 once.

Disc

Work in rnds. At the beginning of every rnd, ch1; at the end of every rnd, join with a sl-st into the first stitch of the rnd. Do not turn work.

Rnd 1: In Red, work 6 sc into an adjustable magic ring. (6 sts)

Rnd 2: [Inc 1] 6 times. (12 sts)

Rnd 3: [1 sc, inc 1] 6 times. (18 sts)

Rnd 4: [2 sc, inc 1] 6 times. (24 sts)

Rnd 5: [3 sc, inc 1] 6 times. (30 sts)

Rnd 6: [4 sc, inc 1] 6 times. (36 sts)

Rnd 7: [5 sc, inc 1] 6 times. (42 sts)

Rnd 8: [6 sc, inc 1] 6 times. (48 sts)

Change to White.

Rnd 9: [7 sc, inc 1] 6 times. (54 sts)

Rnd 10: [8 sc, inc 1] 6 times. (60 sts)

Change to Red.

Rnd 11: [9 sc, inc 1] 6 times. (66 sts)

Rnd 12: [10 sc, inc 1] 6 times. (72 sts)

Change to White.

Rnd 13: [11 sc, inc 1] 6 times. (78 sts)

Break the working yarn, and secure the end.

Following the same instructions, crochet a second piece in Green, but this time, don't break the yarn after Rnd 13. Instead, place both pieces atop each other, right sides facing outward, and crochet them together, working sc through both layers at a rate of 1 sc in every st (78 sts).

Break the working yarn, secure, and weave in the end.

Finishing

- » Place the end of the handle (Rows 31–32) over Rnds 13 and 14 of the disc, and sew it on firmly in basting stitch on both sides of the disc. Break the working yarn, secure, and weave in all ends.

WALKIE-TALKIE

Materials

» #2 fine weight cotton yarn; shown in Woll Butt Camilla, 100% cotton, 138 yd/125 m per 1.75 oz/50 g skein, in colors/amounts as follows:

  » Black, approx 86.7 yd/75 m, 1.1 oz/30 g

  » Grey, approx 15.8 yd/12.5 m, 0.2 oz/5 g

  » Remnants in Red and Green

» Crochet hook, 2.5 mm

» Polyester fiberfill

» Tapestry needle

Walkie-Talkie

Work starts in back-and-forth rows with turning. End every row with ch1; then turn work.

In Black, crochet a chain of 13.

Row 1: Work 1 sc in the 2nd ch from the hook, 1 sc in every following ch. (12 sts)
Rows 2–4: 1 sc in every st of the prev row (12 sts). After having completed the last row, don't turn work.
Continue as follows, working in rnds: At the beginning of every rnd, ch1 and end every round with 1 sl-st into the first st. Do not turn work.
Rnd 5: Crochet an edging around the whole piece, working 38 sc total, of these, 3 sc at each of the 2 sides, 10 sc at each of the top and bottom, and 3 sc into each of the 4 corner sts. (38 sts)
Rnd 6: Working into the back loop of the stitch only, 1 sc in every st of the prev rnd. (38 sts)
Rnds 7–34: 1 sc in every st of the prev rnd. (38 sts)
From here on, work in rows again. End every row with ch1; then turn work.
Row 35: Ch1, turn, working through the front loop of the stitch only, 1 sc in each of next 12 sts. (12 sts)
Rows 36–40: 1 sc in every st of the prev row. (12 sts)
Break the yarn, leaving a long tail.

Stuff the walkie-talkie with fiberfill, and then sew Rows 35–40 to Rnd 34 in overcast stitch.

For better orientation, mark the 4 corners with stitch markers or contrasting yarn before you start seaming.

Antenna

Work in rnds. At the beginning of every rnd, ch1; at the end of every rnd, join with a sl-st into the first stitch of the rnd. Do not turn work.
Rnd 1: In Black, work 6 sc into an adjustable magic ring. (6 sts)
Rnds 2–15: 1 sc in every st of the prev rnd. (6 sts)
Break the yarn, leaving a long tail.

Indicator Lights

Work in rnds. At the beginning of every rnd, ch1; at the end of every rnd, join with a sl-st into the first stitch of the rnd. Do not turn work.
Rnd 1: In Red, work 6 sc into an adjustable magic ring. (6 sts)
Break the yarn, leaving a long tail.
Following the same instructions, crochet another piece in Green.

Triangular Buttons (make 2)

Work in back-and-forth rows with turning. End every row with ch1; then turn work.
In Grey, crochet a chain of 2.
Row 1: Work 2 sc in the 2nd ch from the hook. (2 sts)
Row 2: Inc 1, 1 sc in the next st. (3 sts)
Break the working yarn, leaving a long tail.

Elongated Button

In Grey, crochet a chain of 8.
Rnd 1: Work 1 sc in the 2nd ch from the hook, 1 sc in each of next 5 chains, and 2 sc in the last ch. Continue in the unused loops on the other side of the chain: 1 sc in every ch. Join the rnd with 1 sl-st into the first stitch (14 sts). Break the yarn, leaving a long tail.

Finishing

» Sew the antenna to the top part of the walkie-talkie at the level of Rnds 36–38 in overcast stitch. Sew the 2 indicator lights in basting stitch to the top right of the walkie-talkie at the level of Rnds 32–34. Now, sew the 2 triangular buttons in basting stitch to one narrow side of the walkie-talkie at the level of Rnds 21–24 and Rnds 25–28, with the triangle corners pointing in opposite directions. At the other side, sew on the elongated button at the level of Rnds 21–28 in basting stitch. For the loudspeaker, embroider the front of the walkie-talkie in Grey in running stitch and backstitch over 8 sts each of Rnds 18–24. Break the working yarn, secure, and weave in all ends.

AT THE POLICE STATION

POLICE SHIELD

Materials

» #2 fine weight cotton yarn; shown in Woll Butt Camilla, 100% cotton, 138 yd/125 m per 1.75 oz/50 g skein, in colors/amounts as follows:
  » Grey, approx 15.8 yd/12.5 m, 0.2 oz/5 g
» #2 fine weight cotton yarn; shown in Schachenmayr Catania, 100% cotton, 138 yd/125 m per 1.75 oz/50 g skein, in colors/amounts as follows:
  » Sun or Gold, approx 15.8 yd/12.5 m, 0.2 oz/5 g
» Crochet hook, 2.5 mm
» Tapestry needle

Instructions

Work in rnds. At the beginning of every rnd, ch1; at the end of every rnd, join with a sl-st into the first stitch of the rnd. Do not turn work.

Shield Base

Rnd 1: In Grey, work 6 sc into an adjustable magic ring. (6 sts)
Rnd 2: [Inc 1] 6 times. (12 sts)
Rnd 3: [1 sc, inc 1] 6 times. (18 sts)
Rnd 4: [2 sc, inc 1] 6 times. (24 sts)
Rnd 5: [3 sc, inc 1] 6 times. (30 sts)
Rnd 6: Start with ch3, and then work as follows into the 30 sts of the prev rnd: 2 dc in the first stitch, 1 sc each in the 2nd and 3rd st, 1 hdc in the 4th st, 2 dc in the 5th st, ch2, 1 sc each in the 6th–14th sts, 1 hdc and 1 dc in the 15th st, 1 dc and 1 hdc in the 16th st, 1 sc each in the 17th–25th sts, ch2, 2 dc in the 26th st, 1 hdc in the 27th st, 1 sc each in the 28th and the 29th st, 2 dc in the 30th stitch.
Break the working yarn, secure the end, and weave it in under the sts.

Star

Rnd 1: In either Gold or Sun, work 5 sc into an adjustable magic ring. (5 sts)
Rnd 2: [Inc 1] 5 times. (10 sts)
Rnd 3: [Ch4, 1 sc in the 2nd ch from the hook, 1 hdc in next ch, 1 dc in the last ch, skip 1 st on the ring and work 1 sl-st in the next st of the prev rnd] 5 times.

Finishing

» Break the working yarn, leaving a long tail. Then place star onto the middle of the shield base and sew it on, working in basting stitch.

Tip

Either pin the police shield to the clothing of the child with a safety pin or sew it directly onto the garment as an appliqué.

Thank You!

With this book, a long-fostered dream of mine has come to life.

I would like to thank my family—first and foremost, my husband, for the countless hours he has freed for me so I could concentrate on this project, but also for his motivation and support in so many areas.

Another big thank you goes to my marvelous daughter, who inspired me with countless ideas and has greeted every newly finished piece with radiant eyes. There could be no better motivation imaginable.

Heartfelt thanks also go to my parents, in-laws, and friends, especially to Kathrin, who set me thinking about the whole idea in the first place.

Thank you all for making it possible for me to carry out this undertaking!

Many thanks to the team of EMF Verlag for their confidence in me, especially to Anna Zwicklbauer for the great collaboration and support.